KENT'S UNTOLD HISTORY

Medications, treatments, pills & potions
1650 – 1950

By
Michael Fairley

mifair

First published 2023

Mifair Publishing – Potters Bar, Herts, England

Copyright: Michael Fairley

978-1-3999-7246-8

Typeset in Times 11pt on 18pt

Design by Concept Design

Printed by Kindle Direct Publishing, an Amazon.com company

KENT'S UNTOLD HISTORY

Medications, treatments, pills & potions
1650 – 1950

By
Michael Fairley

mifair

Kent's untold history project

Around three years ago Hawkinge, Kent, author and historian, Michael Fairley, set-out to research and write about what life in Kent was really like at different periods during the 17th, 18th and 19th centuries by creating a series of books on Kent's Untold History. The first five titles in this series have now been published. The aim of the books is to provide answers to the many questions about historic Kent life. Questions such as:

How did people travel around the county two or three hundred years ago? Could prisoners really be convicted and transported to Australia just for stealing three fowls? When were the first railway lines opened in Kent? What kind of music hall performances would theatregoers expect to see in the 1800s? Did medicines really contain opium and other opiates? Was there actually a horse that could do arithmetic and play whist? When did steamships and paddle steamers first start crossing the English Channel? When, and where, was the last person hanged in Kent? Did women ever play football 200 or more years ago?

How long did it take for a stagecoach to travel from Canterbury to London? Were there actually highwaymen and robbers on Kent's main roads? Was the game of cricket played in the 1700s? When did sea bathing first become popular in Kent? What was the Great Horse Manure Challenge? Could bare knuckle boxing matches actually last several hours? Were woman and girls actually burnt at the stake in the county? Did 18th century medicines really claim to 'cure all known ills in the world'? Did horse-drawn bus services really operate in Kent? Was cockfighting a major public sporting activity in Kent?

The answer to all of these intriguing questions can be found in the pages of one or more of the titles already published or in preparation in this historic series. The books provide a fascinating insight into life, travel, theatre, crime and punishment, medicines and medical treatments, sports and pastimes in bygone times – and with a further title in preparation on 'Smuggling, smugglers and contraband.'

Information on all the current books in the Series can be found at the very end of the book.

Preface

Previous books in the 'Kent's Untold History' series have looked at the county's history of crime and punishment, at stagecoach travel and the growth of coaching inns, at sports and recreations, and at music hall and theatre over the past one, two or three hundred years.

This book looks at the changing history of medicines, treatments, pills and potions in Kent from the 17th century onwards, tracing the evolution of medications and drugs prepared by alchemists and doctors from the historically plant-based preparations of the 1600s and 1700s through to the evolution of science-based medicines of the 1900s onwards.

Many of the early medicines contained quite potent, and dangerous, poisons or were tinctures of opium, morphine or cocao in alcohol, with drug addiction becoming a problem that eventually required legislation to control the sale and use of poisons, opiates and similar products and to better protect the public.

Looking at advertisements in Kent newspapers of the time soon finds all kinds of medicines, pills and potions that claimed to cure 'all known ills in the Universe' or 'never known to fail,' or 'provided long lists of satisfied customer' testimonials' effusing about the efficacy of the treatment. The first national pieces of legislation to regulate the sale of medicines was introduced with the 1851 Arsenic Act. This initial Act required that a register had to be kept of all sales, that the buyer had to be known to the seller and that arsenic had to be coloured with a substance such as soot or indigo. A Pharmacy Act followed in 1868

It was not until the early 1900s that controls to regulate the claims made on drug labels were introduced, with pharmaceutical companies finally being required to prove the safety of their drugs, although not yet their efficacy.

Apart from changes in the manufacture, promotion, sale and use of medications, advances were also taking place in the design and manufacture of artificial limbs, many becoming controlled by cables, gears, cranks and springs, which could often be rotated or bent. There were also medical treatments for weak legs or arms and for those with varicose veins.

By the late 1800s new inventions in artificial teeth were also taking place, with advertisements for new types of artificial teeth that could be fitted painlessly without extracting loose teeth or stumps, for enamel for decayed teeth, false teeth with springs, tooth remodelling, lifelike teeth with suction plates, and artificial teeth made with the aid of machinery.

However, it was the late 1800s and early 1900s when some of the most important advances in medication and medical treatments came into being. The discovery of penicillin; advances in surgery, with antiseptic and aseptic surgery that stopped wounds from getting gangrene, as well as operating theatres becoming germ-free environments, and the use of sterilisation to kill bacteria on surgical instruments.

At the end of the 1800s and early 1900s reports and advertisements regarding X-rays were already appearing in Kent newspapers, enabling surgeons to look inside their patients before an operation took place, with X-ray machines being used in hospitals to identify broken or splintered bones and locate dislocated joints. regulations were also introduced to protect operators from scattered radiation, including the wearing of aprons, glasses, gloves and thyroid screens to reduce radiation exposure.

The early 1900s also brought about the discovery of different blood groups and blood compatibility or incompatibility, which showed that blood transfusions would only work if the blood groups were compatible. Like some of the other medical and medicinal developments from the late 1800s and early 1900s, World War I was to act as a key catalyst for the rapid development of blood banks and transfusion techniques, eventually leading to the National Blood Transfusion Service being set up in Britain in 1938.

Probably the most significant advances in healthcare were to come in 1911 and 1948, with, first, the introduction of the National Health Insurance Act, 1911, and then The National Health Service Act introduced on the 5th July 1948, by the Minister of Health, Aneurin Bevan. This later Act was to provide healthcare that was free for all at the point of delivery.

Kent newspapers of course followed all these developments and Acts of Parliament in their pages right through the years of 1911 to 1948, bringing healthcare into a modern world after several hundred years of virtually uncontrolled medicines, unregulated use of poisons and opiates, and with few limits on the reporting of widely exaggerated healthcare successes.

This book in Kent's Untold History series looks at many of these evolutions, development, and discoveries in rather more detail, with input from Kent newspapers in the British Newspaper Archive from the early 1700s right through to the mid 1900s exploring how these advances and changes were implemented.

Contents

THE EARLY TREATMENT OF AILMENTS AND ILLNESSES

Prior to the early 1600s, the treatment of ailments and illnesses was largely based on historical Greek and Roman writings that listed plant materials and their use in medicines. These early texts by the likes of Hippocrates and Aristotle set out that illness arose from an imbalance between what were called the four humours of the body, namely black bile, yellow bile, phlegm and blood. Theory was perhaps more important in the treatment of an illness, rather than direct observation or examination.

Physicians in Kent in the 1600s would look to diagnose a disease by assessing which of the humours was out of alignment and then setting out to treat that illness by removing an excess of that humour (most commonly the chosen approach), or by augmenting what was seen as a weak humour. Some pretty strange courses of treatment were used by physicians to achieve this. Removing an excess of a humour by physical or chemical means was commonly achieved by bloodletting – either by opening a

An early illustration of bloodletting from a vein in the arm

vein (usually in the arm as illustrated) or by using leeches – by sweating, blistering or by administering an enema. Powerful plant-based or other drugs would be used to induce sweating, urination, vomiting or defecation as part of the treatment for an imbalanced humour.

Any ill person that might be lucky enough to escape a bleeding – which could involve taking up to a couple of pints of blood – might be prescribed a drug that included highly toxic compounds such as arsenic and mercury, or some of the natural poisons found in the fields or grown especially for the purpose, like deadly nightshade or hemlock. Indeed, in the 1600s, doctors and apothecaries in Kent were able to draw on a vast store of ancient herbal knowledge with historical texts describing more than 500 plants and their medicinal uses. In the 1700s, herbs were widely used as remedies for all sorts of illnesses, such as dropsy, scrofula, cancer, colic, etc.

APOTHECARIES AND MEDICINAL REMEDIES IN THE 1600S AND 1700s

Apothecaries, which were originally part of the grocery business, had been in existence since the middle ages and, from the early 1600s, used the Pharmacopeia Londinensis published in 1618 as the 'bible' of what could be considered medicinal remedies commonly prescribed by doctors and which apothecaries were required to stock – which ranged from herbs and fruits to minerals and animal and even human products. Backed by King James I, the book was a landmark publication of the College of Physicians, and was the very first list of medicines and their ingredients in England.

Anyone reading the Pharmacopoeia today would probably find the contents rather extraordinary, listing 'medicines' that in the 21st century would be regarded as very unpleasant, even banned. The list

2

included five varieties of urine and fourteen of blood, as well as the saliva, sweat and fat of sundry animals. And not forgetting the 'turds of a goose, of a dog, of a goat, of pigeons, of a stone horse, of a hen, of swallows, of men, of women, of mice, of a peacock, of a hog, and of a heifer.'

Other items that could be found in apothecaries included the penises of stags and bulls, frogs' lungs, castrated cats, ants and millipedes. Perhaps the most bizarre items were discarded nail-clippings (used to provoke vomiting), the skulls of those who had died a violent death (a treatment for epilepsy), and powdered mummy.

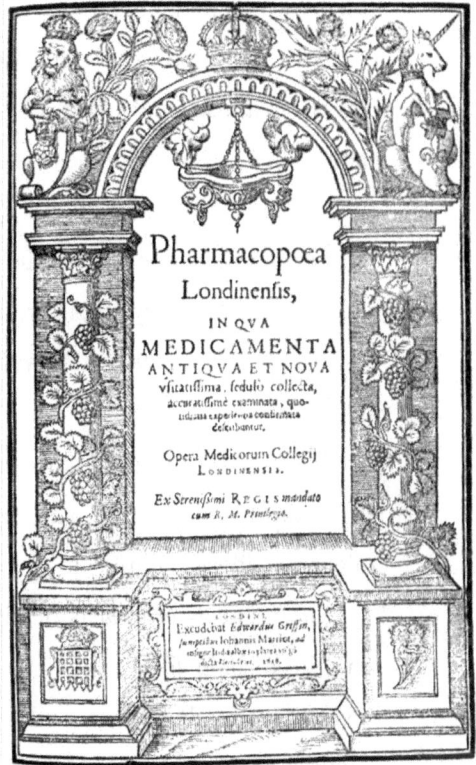

Illustration shows an early copy of the Pharmacopeia Londinensis published in 1618.

At around the same time as the publication of the Pharmacopoeia, the Society for Apothecaries was established in England, breaking away from the Grocers' Company. Recognised publicly by King James I, apothecaries now had a lot more freedom and could sell pretty much whatever they wanted, which ultimately led to the rise of a whole range of quack medicines as doctors, surgeons, alchemists and chemists – as well as all kinds of charlatans made-up and sold their own medicines, pills, creams and potions.

All sorts of strange concoctions appeared in the market, such as oil of swallows and syrup of serpents. Nevertheless, apothecaries and alchemists, despite these very strange concoctions and remedies, undoubtedly enjoyed a golden age during the late 1600s and into the Georgian era of the 1700s and very early 1800s. It was a time of economic prosperity, social reform and scientific discovery, and a period of golden opportunity for developing the business-side of medicine.

By the middle 1800s however, modern more scientific chemistry was starting to develop, and many chemists began leaving the old alchemy ideas behind in favour of developments in scientific research and its emphasis on rigorous quantitative experimentation and its disdain for 'ancient wisdom'. Although the seeds of these events were planted as early as the 17th century, alchemy still flourished for some two hundred years, probably reaching its peak towards the end of 19th century.

THE PREPARATION OF MEDICINES, PILLS AND POTIONS

The methods of preparing medicinal remedies that could be in the form of infusions, tinctures, elixirs, drops, syrups, essences, creams, ointments, serums and pills was, of necessity, quite varied during the 1600 and 1700s. Infusions for example, were boiled for ten minutes over a fire to produce a stronger medicine. Decoctions were produced when boiling might destroy potency, combining the drug with hot water and leaving the mixture to steep for hours or sometimes days.

In some cases, oils, resins or waxes of a plant used for medicines were not water soluble and had to be dissolved in alcohol, resulting in a tincture. Syrups were produced when the plant material was added to water, boiled down and combined with a sweetener like honey which also acted as a preservative. Essential oils could be extracted from botanicals by steam distillation or by soaking large quantities of the plant in small amounts of oil for a long time.

Pills were produced with the necessary combination of the active ingredients, together, often with a liquorice or sugar solution and a filler such as wax, bread dough or gum arabic and then rolling the mixture into strips. These strips would be divided up into small segments by a pharmacist or apothecary using a pill cutter and then each segment finally rolled into a pill shape. Sharp teeth on each edge of the steel pill cutter provided for a different number of pills. One edge gave twelve pills and the other cuts thirty pills. Once cut and shaped, the pills were then hardened, coated and stored.

Tinctures, as already mentioned, were liquid extracts of herbs, usually made with alcohol or vinegar. They were widely used as health remedies for various diseases and conditions throughout the 1700s. Indeed, Laudanum, a tincture of opium, was considered as a wonder drug in the 1700s and 1800s. It contained almost all opium alkaloids, including morphine and codeine and was used as a pain medication and cough suppressant, as well as to treat many other conditions.

Some other examples of tinctures from that time included toad and mercury, while. a popular tincture in 1700s Kent was sold in numerous town outlets as Basil Valentin's Cordial Tincture of Gold, but more of this particular medication in a later chapter.

Elixirs were sweet liquids containing at least one active ingredient that was used medicinally to cure an illness. They were taken orally. Tasteless Ague and Fever Drops were another popular remedy in Kent during the 1700s. Advertising for this medication stated that the drops were 'the most efficacious medicine in the world for the Ague and Intermittent Fever.'

An early recipe for 'True Daffy,' an elixir from the 1700s listed the following ingredients: aniseed, brandy, cochineal, elecampane, fennel seed, jalap, manna, parsley seed, raisin, rhubarb, saffron, senna and Spanish Liquorice (supposedly because Spanish monks grew liquorice). Subsequent chemical analysis has shown True Daffy to be a laxative made mostly from alcohol. Other elixir recipes include the resin of Guaiacum wood chips, caraway, Salt of Tartar, and scammony (a bindweed native to the eastern Mediterranean).

Syrups and electuaries were also widely used remedies for coughs in the 1600s. Some of the ingredients included conserve of red roses, balsam of sulphur, powdered frankincense, oil of vitriol, the milk of sow thistle, and syrup of coltsfoot. Opiates were again common ingredients and were used to induce sedation.

Serums at this time were substances that were applied to the skin to improve its appearance or health. In the 1700s, some common skincare cosmetics were face tomers (toners), scented waters, and cold cream made with oils, wax, and rosewater. Serums were also sometimes referred to as liquids that contained antibodies or antigens that were used to treat or prevent diseases. In the 1700s, there was no scientific understanding of how serums worked, and most diseases were treated with herbal remedies, bloodletting, or surgery.

Another quite popular treatment in Kent at the end of the 1700s was Whiteheads Essence of Mustard which was prepared and sold in both pill and liquid state at 2s. 9d. for each box or bottle and carried the signature of the Patent holder, Mr. R. Johnston (an apothecary and chemist in London), in his own hand.

Treatments could also be external. Creams and ointments were herbal oils combined with beeswax or fat to produce a compound which was solid at room temperature. Compresses, poultices and plaisters (plasters) were plant materials applied externally, usually in combination with heat or moisture.

Probably the most crucial period of medical preparation development was during the 1800s, particularly in terms of their potency. Victorians quite widely took to taking alcohol and opium, but also to cocao and mescal. The chemists of this time not only sold proprietary medicines but made nostrums themselves from raw ingredients to create their own home remedies, such as laudanum for dysentery or camphorated tincture of opium for asthma.

There are also reports of opium pills that were coated in varnish for the working classes, silver coated for the rich, and gold for the very rich. Some Pectoral medications for children also contained a mixture of alcohol and opium – a mixture more likely to be classified as a poison today.

With the invention of the hypodermic needle in the 1840s, it was not just opium being used in medications, but morphine and heroin as well, eventually leading to the beginnings of drug control, as well as the medicalisation of those that became addicted to these powerfully potent substances.

THE RISE OF PATENT MEDICINES

Patent medicines, also known as proprietary medicines, were secret remedies and homemade formulas developed by alchemists, chemists, surgeons or doctors, who applied for and were granted a monopoly in the market by the English crown. First created in the 17th century, patent medicines were non-prescription medical preparations that were protected and could be found advertised in English and Kent newspapers under a trademark and trade name from quite early in the 1700s. No publicity or marketing gimmick was missed in their promotion: no cure, no money; bargain packs, free pamphlets with every purchase or a silver measuring spoon, sugar-coated pills, violin-shaped bottles, treatment gratis for unfortunates or soldiers returning from the wars, and so forth.

Such medications were mass-produced and became widely used and popular during the mid-to-late 1700s and through the 1800s and 1900s. Many became brand name best sellers, although quite often containing harmful or ineffective ingredients.

Newspapers were undoubtedly a vital element in the sale of medicines and pills, providing not just publicity but also key sales outlets. Newspaper offices acted as depots for their sale, and newspaper deliverers often routinely delivered parcels of pills, medicines or creams. The links between quacks and the publishing industry were intimate, even insidious. Indeed, the printing works of the *Kentish Weekly Post* or *Canterbury Journal*, in St. Margaret's, Canterbury, were a veritable sales outlet for all kinds of medical products in the 1700s and 1800s.

Some of the earliest patented medicines that were advertised in the Kent newspapers and sold through their offices or printing works during the 1720s, 1730s and 1740s, include Daffy's Elixir; Dr. Bateman's and Dr. Newman's Pectoral Drops (whose original patent was granted by King George I in 1726); Dr. Geoffrey's Cordial Sugar Plums; Chymical water to cure the itch; Dr. John Hooper's Female Pills, described as the most useful remedy against those general complaints that the female sex is subjected to; 'The Famous Purging Sugar Pills' universally esteemed for bringing away worms; Delescot's original Conferes of Myrtle Opiate for cleansing, whitening and preserving teeth and making the gums most beautifully red; or Chase's Balsamic Pills – a certain and immediate cure for all manner of pains occasioned by colds settled in the head, body and limbs; as well as Spirits of Scurvy Grass, and Cephalic snuff for the head. More information on these, and other early medications, will appear in subsequent chapters.

Largely originating in England as medicines that were manufactured under grants, or 'patents of royal favour' these patent medicines, because there were no drug laws in the USA until after the turn of the 19th Century, enabled English pharmacists and doctors to start manufacturing and mass producing their own patent drugs and shipping them to the States during the late 18th century with no interference from any government or state agencies.

Indeed, it is said that the English market at this time was flooded with more than 200 patent cure-all elixirs, pills, ointments and serums, many with their own proprietary brand names and secret formulas which were packaged and labelled in distinctive medicine bottles, tins or boxes of the time. This was perhaps the real beginning

A selection of patented and 'quack' pills, ointments and creams dating from the middle 1800s.

of 'Branding' in Europe. Any claim for a drug could be made without any kind of credentials.

Many of these earliest patent English medications later proved to be very successful with the American colonies and were exported in great volumes. Indeed, some of these early patented medications, such as Bateman's Pectoral Drops even survived well into the 20th century. Many of the innovators of these patent and 'quack' medicines gained a fortune and became very rich.

Botanical remedies remained important medicinally through the 1700s and early 1800s However, by the middle of the 19th century, organic chemists were already beginning to isolate specific active ingredients in medicinal plants. Even so, some 80% of pharmaceuticals were still derived from botanical sources by 1900. This would soon change. Due to cost of production and storage, as well as the varied concentration of an

Drug discoveries in the 19th and 20th centuries:

Morphine	**c1803**
Quinine	**1820**
Aspirin	**1853**
Paracetamol	**1877**
Amphetamine	**1887**
Adrenaline	**1901**
Thyroxine	**1915**
Insulin	**1921**
Penicillin	**1928**

active ingredient from locale to locale and even from plant to plant, drug companies such as Smith, Kline French, Beecham's, Bayer and Roche had been formed in the USA, England and Europe in the 1800s. These companies developed new products (Aspirin by Bayer, and Beecham's Pills) or concentrated on replicating cheaper synthetic drugs.

Early remedies that started to arrive in America from England with the early settlers included John Hooper's Female Pills, Dr Bateman's Pectoral Drops, and Daffy's Elixir Salutis for 'colic and

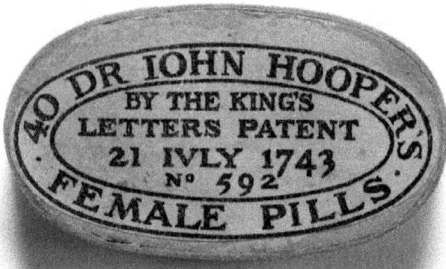

Dr. John Hooper's Female Pills, widely sold in England and America for well over 100 years.

griping.' These medicines were sold to the public through early grocers, tailors, goldsmiths, newspaper offices, and other local merchants, as well as being extensively marketed with editorial-type advertisements in the national and local newspapers of the time. Such remedies were available for almost any kind of ailment, including tuberculosis, indigestion, gout, venereal disease and even tumours and cancer.

CHEMISTS HOMEMADE REMEDIES

During the Victorian era chemists stocked not only the many patent and proprietary medicines that were ready made, but nostrums made by themselves from raw ingredients for their own homemade remedies. These included laudanum for dysentery, chlorodyne for coughs and colds, and camphorated tincture of opium for asthma.

Even so, up until 1916, drug use in England was largely uncontrolled and drugs incorporating opium, morphine, heroin and coca were relatively commonplace and widely used. It was not until the provisions of the Dangerous Drugs Acts of 1920 and 1923 were introduced and regulated the distribution of opioid supplies and controlled illicit supplies; a policy maintained in Britain until the 1960s. Subsequent legislation on the use and control of rugs has been introduced in more recent years.

Regulations were also introduced to regulate the claims made on drug labels and pharmaceutical companies were finally required to prove the safety of their drugs – although not yet the efficacy.

DRUG COMPANIES FOUNDED IN THE 1800S.

Many of the major drug companies – still known today – got their early start by selling and/or producing patent medicines or other early healthcare products. Smith, Kline & French for example was founded in 1830. Beecham's Pills were launched in 1842. Bayer started selling aspirin in 1863. Roche healthcare came about in 1896. It is perhaps worth exploring a little more about the history and evolution of some of these early drug giants.

The story of the drug companies starts in 1830, when

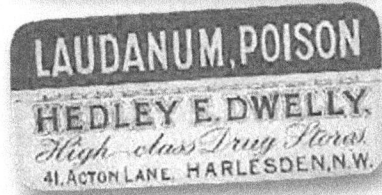

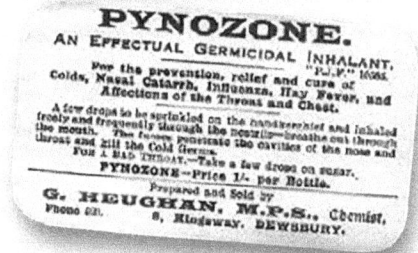

MEDICINAL ALUM

G. HEUGHAN M.P.S.
DISPENSING CHEMIST,
8.KINGSWAY. DEWSBURY.
TEL.593.

SYRUP OF SQUILLS

James A. White, M.P.S.
CHEMIST & PHARMACIST,
63 BRADFORD ROAD, SHIPLEY.
157 BRADFORD ROAD,
TELEPHONE Nº 422.

LAUDANUM, POISON

HEDLEY E. DWELLY,
High class Drug Stores
41.ACTON LANE. HARLESDEN, N.W.

PYNOZONE.
AN EFFECTUAL GERMICIDAL INHALANT.
"P.J.F." 1695.
For the prevention, relief and cure of
Colds, Nasal Catarrh, Influenza, Hay Fever, and
Affections of the Throat and Chest.
A few drops to be sprinkled on the handkerchief and inhaled
freely and frequently through the nostrils—breathe out through
the mouth. The fumes penetrate the cavities of the nose and
throat and kill the Cold Germs.
FOR A BAD THROAT.—Take a few drops on sugar.
PYNOZONE—Price 1/- per Bottle.
Prepared and Sold by
G. HEUGHAN, M.P.S., Chemist,
Phone 22. 8, Kingsway. DEWSBURY.

TELEPHONE Nº 422.
OIL OF WINTERGREEN
(ARTIFICIAL)
FOR EXTERNAL USE ONLY

James A. White, M.R.S.
CHEMIST & PHARMACIST,
63 BRADFORD ROAD, SHIPLEY.
157 BRADFORD ROAD,

Some examples of chemists' nostrums from the early 1900s

13

John K Smith opened his first drugstore in Philadelphia, USA, and sold drugs, paint, varnish and window glass. Eleven years later, John retired and his son George took on the company, which then became John K Smith & amp, Co. Mahlon Kline joined Smith and Shoemaker (as it had become by 1865) as a bookkeeper, after studying business at college. Throughout the next ten years, Mahlon took on additional responsibilities within the company and was rewarded when the company was renamed as Smith, Kline and Company.

It was around the same time, that Thomas Beecham launched the Beecham's Pills laxative business in England. In 1859, Beecham opened a factory in St Helens – the world's first factory to be built solely for making medicines. Beecham's Pills were advertised as acting like magic on a weak stomach, impaired digestion and disorders of the liver. By the 1890s, Beecham's Pills were being promoted as having the largest sale of any patented medication in the world. The first for making medicines wasn't the company's only first – in 1887, Beecham's factory was the first in the area to have electricity.

In Germany, the Bayer chemical and pharmaceutical company was founded in 1863, starting out as a small dyestuffs factory in Barmen. They discovered how to make the dye fuchsine, bringing Aspirin to the market in 1899.

The Roche company was founded in Switzerland, Germany and Italy in 1896 by Fritz Hoffmann-La Roche as one of the first companies specifically set up to manufacture scientifically researched pharmaceuticals. Hoffmann-La Roche recognized that the industrial manufacture of medicines would be a major advance in the fight against disease and focused his company on innovation and establishing and international presence.

Meanwhile in New Zealand, Englishman Joseph Nathan established a general trading company called Joseph Nathan & Co. By 1904, the company began exporting dried milk powder to London, which was trademarked as Glaxo two years later. In 1908, the Glaxo department of Joseph Nathan & Co. opened in London.

Back in the USA, Smith Kline and Company increased its portfolio of consumer brands by acquiring French, Richards and Company. In 1910, a range of iron tablets, lozenges and poison ivy lotion, called the Blue Line, was added to the company – then called Smith, Kline and French. Nine years later, Mahlon Kline began sending pharmaceutical samples through the mail to doctors across the US.

Glaxo's first pharmaceutical product was the vitamin D preparation, Ostelin, in 1924. The company built new research facilities in 1935, called Glaxo Laboratories, which absorbed Joseph Nathan & Co. in 1947. In the same year, Glaxo was listed for the first time on the London Stock Exchange. More than a century and many new formations and mergers, Glaxo Wellcome acquired SmithKline Beecham in 2000 to form GlaxoSmithKline.

NEW DEVELOPMENTS IN MEDICATED WOUND CARE

As far back as 1880, Paul Beiersdorf in Germany took over a chemist's shop in Muhlenstrasse and, working in close co-operation with Dr. Oscar Troplowitz, developed a process to manufacture self-adhesive medical plasters, registering the first patent in 1882. This was the foundation of the Beiersdorf company. By 1892, the factory manufactured branded goods such as Labello and Nivea, as well as medical plasters and pharmaceutical products. The company also worked on self-adhesive bandages. In 1931, after signing an agreement with Smith & Nephew, Beiersdorf gained the right to manufacture and distribute medical plasters in the UK.

Meanwhile, in 1920s America, Earle Dickinson, a cotton buyer at Johnson & Johnson, was developing Band-Aid bandages, putting squares of cotton gauze at selected intervals along an adhesive strip, and then covering them with crinoline to protect them and stop them sticking together. Then in 1938, the company introduced self-adhesive bandages, millions of which were to be used to treat injured soldiers during World War II.

A BRIEF INTRODUCTION TO VETERINARY MEDICINE

It is not possible to determine when veterinary medicine first began, but it probably dates back to the early domestication of animals many thousands of years ago. Having said that, it was not undertaken with any great seriousness in Europe until the 1700s. An early reference to veterinary medication can be found in the *Kentish Weekly Post* or *Canterbury Journal* from 30th January 1754. This stated that 'A very singular specific against the distemper that reigns amongst the cattle has been tried in the neighbourhood, and tried with success where the inflammation was not too far advanced: They took the guts of any beast that died of distemper, dried and reduced them to powder, made them up into pills and gave them to cattle as soon as they are infected with the disorder.'

Specific Medications for Cattle and Horses were nevertheless being sold in the *Kentish Gazette* as early as 1783, with advertising of the following treatments: Dr. James's Powder; Ragley's horse medications, viz, purging, diuretic, and Saffron Balls; worm, fever and pectoral powders; rhubarb physic; and dog balls.

The first veterinary educational institute in Europe was not founded until 1762, with Louis XV of France establishing a Royal School of veterinarian medicine in France in 1765. The London Veterinary College was founded in1791, with the Royal College of Veterinary Surgeons being set-up by royal charter in 1844.

Records from the *Kentish Weekly Post* or *Canterbury Journal* of September 1796, show that a meeting was held at the Fountain Tavern, Canterbury, for the establishment of a Veterinary Hospital, on rational and scientific principles, for the benefit of the community at large. Various resolutions were passed, a subscription rate of two guineas established, subscribers entered and a bank account established, with the date for a general meeting of the Hospital put in the diary.

Veterinary care and management were now usually led by a veterinary surgeon or 'vet' - a Doctor of Veterinary Medicine or veterinary medical doctor, a role equivalent to a physician or surgeon (medical doctor) in human medicine, and involving postgraduate study and qualification.

Veterinary science is said to have really come of age from the later years of the 1800s and in to the early years of the 1900s. It was at this time that the treatment of horses, cattle, pigs, dogs and sheep was also beginning, with everything from liniments for cuts and bruises, sprains, sore backs and shoulders, to condition powders.

Examples of veterinary products labels for White Oils and Condition Powders, both dating from the early 1900s, are shown in the following two illustrations. These two products are being variously specified on the labels as being for use with horses, cattle, dogs and sheep.

It was not only farm animal medications that were being produced from the early 1900s, there were also treatments for destroying the vermin that were infesting barns, granaries and Barn Yards, with mice and rats devouring the corn in such large volumes that it equated to all the seed required to sow the ensuing year's crop. An extract from a promotional document of the time is summarized as follows.

'Over 200 or more years the medical treatment of men, women and children, as well as horses, cattle, sheep and dogs has changed from the early quack medications of the 1600s and 1700s to more science and anatomical-based treatments from the 1800 onwards. The following pages of this publication explore these changes, the new medications and treatments, and move to new decades of controls and safety as medication moved into the 20th century.

PROPRIETARY MEDICINES FROM THE LATE 1600S AND EARLY 1700S

The earliest Kent newspapers that are archived in the British Newspaper Archive date from 1726. Even at this time, newspapers such as the *Kentish Weekly Post* or *Canterbury Journal* already carried various, and sometimes quite numerous, advertisements for patented, proprietary or quack medicines, often promising remedies that would cure an extremely wide and diverse range of illnesses and ailments. Nearly all these medicines were available for initial purchase from the newspaper's Printing Offices in Canterbury, and then later from grocery shops, postal offices, chemists and other outlets throughout Kent.

One of the very earliest of these proprietary medicines advertised regularly in the newspaper over several decades, commencing in March 1726, was for Dr. Anderson's famous Scot's Pills. 'Prepared under his

> Dr. *ANDERSON*'s, or
> The Famous *SCOT'S* PILLS;
> ARE faithfully prepared only by JAMES INGLISH, Son of DAVID INGLISH, deceased, at the Unicorn, over-against the New Church in the Strand, London; and to prevent Counterfeits from Scotland, as well as in and about London, you are desired to take Notice, That the true Pills have their Boxes sealed on the Top (in Black Wax) with a Lyon Rampant, and Three Mullets Argent, Dr. Anderson's Head betwixt I, I. with his Name round it, and Isabella Inglish underneath the Shield in a Scroll. They are of excellent Use in all Cases where Purging is necessary, and may be taken with Epsom, Tunbridge, or other Medicinal Waters.

Majesty's authority by James Inglish at the Unicorn, against the New Church in the Strand, London, and sold at the printing Office in Canterbury.' The advertisement added that Scot's Pills were 'Universally known and approved by eminent physicians and others of all ranks for their rare and singular virtues; were very convenient for all travellers by sea and land. Priced at one shilling each box. A paper of its virtues and directions given with each box.'

Dr. Anderson was an Edinburgh-born (in 1579) physician to his

Majesty King Charles I, as well as being constantly used as a physick by Charles II. Anderson's Scot's Pills (also known as Scots Pills), were mildly aperient pills that contained aloes, colocynth and gamboge (a Southeast Asian tree resin used as a colouring vehicle and cathartic in early medicines), and were sold as a remedy for cleansing the system after over-indulgence. They were first marketed as the 1630s, eventually being left to posterity when Anderson died around 1660. Scot's then continued to be prepared by an I Inglish who was living at the Unicorn in the Strand. He was followed by grandson, David Inglish, and later by James Inglish.

WONDERFUL CURES AND POPULAR MEDICATIONS

Another medication regularly advertised in the *Kentish Weekly Post* or *Canterbury Journal*, again from 1726, was Bateman's Pectoral Drops. In April of that year, the newspaper printed an announcement that King George I, having been made aware of the 'surprising efficacy of Bateman's Pectoral Drops, with the wonderful cures made by the same, on some of his own household, and thousands of others of his loving subjects in the several parts of Great Britain: To prevent counterfeits and secure the property to Benjamin Okell, the sole inventor and to John Cluer, Robert Raikes and Wm Dicey, the persons concerned with him, His Majesty has been pleased to grant his Letters Patents, under the Great Seal of Great Britain.'

With a Royal Patent, Bateman's Pectoral Drops became a very popular medication for disorders of the chest or lungs, not only in the early 1700s, but right through to the early 20th centuries in both Britain and America. It was subsequently also marketed as a remedy for all rheumatic and chronic complaints, including pains of the limbs, bones, joints, as well as for influenza and violent colds.

As part of an advertisement for the Drops in the *Kentish Weekly Post* or *Canterbury Journal* of 22nd April, 1743, it carried the following testimonial:

Please to assure the Persons who serve you with Dr, Bateman's PECTORAL DROPS, that having frequently been with Rheumatick Pains in a most terrible Manner, at length grew so bad therewith, that the Use of my Limbs was taken from me, and I was hardly ever out of Bed for six Months, my Life being entirely despair'd of, as nothing which could be apply'd gave me Ease, and the Pains still more violent; at which Time a Neighbour, who had found Comfort by taking Dr. Bateman's PECTORAL DROPS, advised a Dose thereof, which in a very short Time gave me some Ease and Sleep, which I had long been without; and finding such Success from the first Dose, I continued taking thereof, and before I had completed the Quantity of five Shillings-worth, I was perfectly free from all Pain and my Strength, &c. came to me In a sudden, and, I may say, miraculous Manner, that I think myself obliged, for the general Advancement of the Afflicted, to desire that my Case as above may be made publick.

I am your Obliged and Humble Servant, JOHN CLARK.

It was said to work chiefly 'to moderate Sweat and Urine, exceeding all other Medicines yet found out for the Rheumatism, and highly successful under the afflictions of Stones and Gravel, Pains, Agues, Colds.' The regular newspaper advertisements all concluded with the following: 'N. B. The aforesaid Dr. Bateman's Pectoral Drops continue to be Sold at the Printing Office, Canterbury, at twelve pence each bottle.'

Pectoral Drops were not the only medication under the Bateman name in the 1720. Many regular Kent newspaper advertisements also promoted Bateman's famous Spirits of Scurvy Grass, noting that this plain spirit was 'an excellent way of Prevention, where the Scorbutick Humour is not yet grown too strong. It gives any liquor a pleasing taste, cheers the Spirits, Warms and comforts the Stomach and thereby creates a good Appetite, and helps Digestion.'

Later in the advertisement it added 'Tis a rare Remedy to sweeten and cure an Offensive Breath. It prevents worms in Children, it cuts, attenuates and dissolves Flegm and Crudities contrived by large Suppers, or over drinking, and helps those that are troubled with Wind, Vapour, and sour Belching. It cuts off and disperses causes of Scurvy, Dropsies, and many other diseases in the bud, and is a grand preservative of health if often used. Many people never drink Morning Draught without it, and find great Benefit. You may take Thirty or Forty Drops in Half a pint of Beer, Ale, Cyder, or other Liquors, at any Time, an Hour before or after Meats, but in the Morning is the most proper.'

It also noted that 'The Golden Spirit is used when the Scurvy is red coloured and become dangerous and where Purging is necessary to which Purpose it is impregnated with choice ingredients most friendly to Nature. It is also an excellent and sovereign medicine in the Dropsy. Gout, Stone and Gravel, Melancholy, Greensickness, and several other Diseases, as in the particular Directions for its Use, is truly and more at large set forth. Price of each bottle One shilling.'

A GREAT PRESERVER OF MANKIND WITH NO BETTER REMEDY IN THE WORLD

In December 1726 the *Kentish Weekly Post* or *Canterbury Journal* printed an advertisement (shown here courtesy British Newspaper Archive) for Dr. Daffey's Original and Famous Cordial 'Elixir Salutis.' It was noted as 'The great Preserver of Mankind, and stating that with over 60 years experience, it is a certain cure (under God) in most Distempers, The Gout and Rheumatism, with all those torturing pains attending them; it takes away the scurvy root and branch, and gives immediate ease in the most racking pain of the Chollick.'

The advertisement continued with 'It is a sovereign and never failing remedy against Fluxes, Spitting of Blood, Consumption, Agues, Small Pox, and Measles; it carries off the small violent

Truly Prepared at London, and appointed to be sold at no other Place in Canterbury but at the PRINTING Office,

Dr. DAFFEY's

Original and Famous Cordial Elixir Salutis; The Great Preserver of Mankind; above 80 Years Experienced. It is a certain Cure (under God) in most Distempers, viz. The Gout and Rheumatism, with the Pains attending them; takes away the Scurvy Root and Branch, and gives immediate Ease in the most racking Pains of the Cholick. It is a sovereign and never failing Remedy against Fluxes, spitting of Blood, Consumptions, Agues, Small-Pox and Measles; it carries off the most violent Fevers, eases After-Pains, prevents Miscarriages; cures the Rickets in Children: is wonderful in the Stone and Grave, in the Kidneys, Bladder or Ureter, and brings away Slime, Gravel, and often-times Stones of great bigness; for Stoppages or Pains in the Head and Heart, a better Remedy in the World cannot be; it perfectly destroys Worms to a Miracle, cureth the Black or Yellow Jaundice, King's Evil, and those who are stopt with Flegm, restoring a languishing Body to perfect Health, strengthning the Vessels of both Sexes, cleansing the whole Mass of Blood. A noble Cordial after hard drinking.

fevers; eases after pains, prevents miscarriages, curing the Ricketts in Children; its wonderful in the Stone and Gravel; for stoppages or pains in the Stomach, shortness of breath, Pains in the Head, then a better remedy in the World cannot be; it perfectly destroys worms, and careth the black or yellow Jaundice.' It again states that the medication is only available at the Printing Offices in St. Margaret's in Canterbury.

A footnote to the advertisement added that: 'This choice cordial preserved hundreds of families in the dreadful Plague at London in 1665. Recommended to all families. Priced 2s. 6d. the large half pint, and 1s. 3d. the quarter pint, with printed directions at large for taking.'

By 1729, the same newspaper is carrying advertisements for Dr. Eaton's Balsamick Styptick, noting that this Medicine 'stops all bleedings, whether inward or outward, proceeding either from Bruises, Sprains, Bursting of Veins, Wounds, or other causes whatsoever, and is a ready Help in time of great Danger or Distress, very proper to be had by Apothecaries, Surgeons, and Midwives, and by every Family, especially such as have not a Physician or Surgeon at Hand. Price 2s. 6d. Bottle. Note, The few Bottle that remain, were prepared by the doctor's own Hands.'

KILLS ALL SORT OF WORM IN HUMAN BODIES

In 1729, the *Kentish Weekly Post* or *Canterbury Journal* starts carrying regular advertisements for 'Dr. Richard Rock's Famed Stomach Plaister for Curing all forms of AGUES and Intermitting fevers, as hundreds of Men, Women and Children can testify, who have been wonderfully cured in a short time.' The advertisement stated that the Plaister cures swell'd Bellies in Children in less than 24 Hours, without any other Medicines; kills and destroys all sorts of Worms in human bodies; gives present Relief in the Cholick, Phisick or Shortness of Breath; which it accomplishes without any Trouble or Disorder to either Sex, strengthening and comforting the Stomach, and is so safe that Women with Child may apply it with safety. It likewise cures Loathing Sickness and Reachings in the Morning, and creates an Appetite.'

By way of recommendation the advert also carried the following message:

Mrs. Heneage's Daughter, Living within a few Doors of the Royal Oak at Chatham, was troubled with a Pain of her Stomach and Shortness of Breath, and by applying the plaister to her Stomach, was freed from the Pain, and parted from three sorts of Worms.

This was followed by a second testimonial:

A Servant of Mr. Baxter, a Bricklayer, living in East Lane, in Maidstone, was Cured of an Ague and fever by this Plaister.

The advertisement finally noted: 'Beware of Counterfeits, it is sold at no other Place in Kent. Price 6d. with Directions at large. Sold at the Printing Office in St. Margaret's, Canterbury, and by the men who carry the Canterbury News Paper.

It should also be noted that apart from his stomach plaisters, Richard Rock (1690 to 1777) was a well-known doctor practicing in 18th century London. In the 1730s, Dr. Rock was also advertising Dr. Rock's Tincture for giving ease in the toothache, curing scurvy in the gums, and making the foulest teeth as white as ivory. Price one shilling a bottle. He was equally famous for his remedy for venereal disease.

25

THE MOST USEFUL REMEDY FOR COMPLAINTS OF THE FEMALE SEX

It was in 1743 that one of the most widely advertised and promoted medications of the 1700s and 1800s, namely Dr. John Hooper's Female Pills, arrived and was granted the King's Letters of Patent, signed by John, Archbishop of Canterbury. In the Patent letter, addressed to the Public, it set out why the patent had been granted, stating that: 'These pills, by long experience in private practice, have been found the useful remedy against those general complaints that the Female Sex are subjected to: they cleanse, purify, and cause a free circulation of the blood, when in a manner stagnant, open those obstructions which Virgins are so liable to and bring nature into its proper channel, whereby health is revived, and the Patient that looked like death restored to a lively complexion.'

Later in the advertisement it went on to describe the Female Pills as 'the best Medicine ever discovered for young women when afflicted with what is vulgarly called the Green Sickness, which one or two boxes will certainly cure; also good for Palpitations of the Heart, Giddiness, Fainting, Loathing of Food, Bad Digestion, Pains of the Stomach, a beating of the Arteries in the Neck, Short Breath upon every little motion, sinking of the Spirits, a dejected Countenance, and a dislike to conversation, and likewise for the Scurvy.'

If this glowing review wasn't enough, the advertisement went further by adding: 'For all distempers they are most excellent, and are to be given from seven to seventy years old. They are likewise equally proper for married women, unless with child, and ought always to be taken one month after delivery, for they cleanse the womb and purge of those gross humours which, when retained, generate numerous diseases, and render women unhealthy all their lives, and for this reason, they should always be taken at the age of Forty-five, or Fifty.'

Each advertisement concluded with: 'Each box contains 40 pills, which is about 10 doses, and are sealed up inside their directions with a seal (illustrated) having the words, JN HOOPER'S FEMALE PILLS, and round it, BY THE KING'S PATENT, the same as in the margin. Price one shilling the Box. These pills are appointed to be sold at the Printing Office in St. Margaret's, Canterbury, and may be had by speaking to the Newsmen.'

A CERTAIN AND IMMEDIATE CURE

In 1749 a new advertiser appears regularly in the *Kentish Weekly Post* or *Canterbury Journal*, this time to promote CHASE'S Balsamick Pills, developed by the advertisement author in his private practice as a Man Midwife and Apothecary, and now available for general good. Chase's Pills were said to be 'a certain

---

CHASE's *Balfamick Pills.*

M Any Years experienced by the Author, in his private Practice, as a Man Midwife and Apothecary, at *Luton* in *Bedfordshire*, are now published for a general Good. —— The uncommon Succels which daily attends their being taken, in different Dilorders, Ages, and Conflitutions, fufficiently proves them to be

A Certain and Immediate CURE

---

and immediate cure for all manner of pains occasioned by Colds in the Head, Body and Limbs, or any of their parts, as the Eyes, Ears, Throat, Shoulders, Sides, Back and Loins.

Other claims made for the Pills included the curing of all manner of coughs; for Asthma, and all other disorders of the lungs; for all inward bruises, and spitting of blood; for the bloody flux and diarrhoea; for all kinds of chollick in the stomach or bowels; for gout and rheumatism; for fevers and agues; for eruptick fevers such as small-pox and chicken-pox; for hooping cough, and gripes in children.

Special mention is also made of the benefits the Pills provide in preventing Miscarriages, saying that they are the most necessary medicine that can be given to women after a sharp and difficult labour, instantly relieving, as well as preventing those acute pains and weakness that frequently succeed upon a critical birth; therefore, as an excellent succour in those cases, it is necessary they should be kept in readiness by all careful midwives and nurses.

Like Dr. Hooper's Female Pills, the pills sold by Chase were supplied in boxes and sealed, this time with Chase's Coat of Arms. Priced at 2s a box, each box containing six doses of pills. Only available in Kent at the Printing Office in Canterbury.

Associated with the advertisement for Chase's Balsamick Pills was a follow-on advertisement for Delecot's Conserve of Myrtle, 'available in Europe for nearly fifty years for cleansing, whitening and preserving the teeth, making the gums most beautifully red, and leaving a sweat breath. Price two shillings and six-pence for a small Gally-Pot, with directions. Also available, the root of Dragon's Blood, that is used instead of a brush. Price one shilling. Again, available from the Printing Office Canterbury.'

THE SMALLEST, PLEASANTEST AND SAFEST MEDICINE EVER OFFERED TO THE PUBLIC

Appearing regularly in the *Kentish Weekly Post* or *Canterbury Journal* from March 1748, an advertisement (illustrated courtesy of British Newspaper Archive) for The Rev. Mr. Clendon's Fever Pill, or Powder, noted that the medication 'Cured effectually all sorts of Fevers, and usually in just a few hours, and numbers more are ready to certify, but also ready to attest the same upon Oath.'

It went on to say that 'It is the smallest, the pleasantest, and the safest Medicine, that ever was offered to the Public; and what makes it yet more valuable, it is best to take it when the Fever rages most; whereas the Bark, taken at such a time, often proves of dangerous, and sometimes fatal Consequence. And as for Agues, tho' of never so long standing, they are easily cured by it.

'Many have taken it so happily in the Symptoms of the Small Pox, that it is suppos'd, whoever takes it in due time will have them favourably, without suffering the dreadful Havock that Distemper often makes with fine Faces

The Rev. Mr. *CLENDON's* Fever Pill, or Powder,

CURES effectually all forts of Fevers, and ufually in a few Hours, as many have certify'd in the Public Papers, and Numbers more are not only ready to certify, but alfo ready to atteft the fame upon Oath, is defired.

It is the fmalleft, the pleafanteft, and the fafeft Medicine, that ever was offered to the Public; and what makes it yet more valuable, it is beft to take it when the Fever rages moft; whereas the Bark, taken at fuch a time, often proves of dangerous, and fometimes fatal Confequence. And as for Agues, tho' of never fo long ftanding, they are eafily cured by it.

Many have taken it fo happily in the Symptoms of the Small Pox, that it is fuppos'd, whoever takes it in due time will have them favourably, without fuffering the dreadful Havock that Diftemper often makes with fine Faces.

If any Perfon within thefe feven Years laft paft has taken it without Succefs, the Author defires that Perfon to advertife the fame, provided he was not afflicted with other Diforders at the fame time ; and if all have been Cured who have taken it, Is it not a Specific worthy the publick Cognizance.

Each Twelve-penny Box, containing ufually enough to cure three or four Perfons, and fometimes as many more, with printed Directions, to prevent Counterfeits, is fealed with the Author's own Butt, and thefe Words, The Rev. Mr. Clendon.

Let this Medicine but have Juftice done it, and then its Author does not fear but he fhall meet with the general Approbation for thus ftrenuoufly promoting the Ufe of it.

Thefe Pills (which never lofe their Virtue, if kept dry) are appointed by the Author to be fold at the Printing-Office in Canterbury, by Wholefale and Retail, with Directions and Certificates of Cures.

They are alfo Sold by Retail at Mrs. Drayfon's, Shop keeper in Faverfham.

NB. Numbers whom Mr. *Clendon* has Cured of the King's Evil, Leprofy, and Deafnefs, may be feen, but no Names ask'd, at his Houfe in *Bolt-Court, in Fleetftreet, London,* on proper Notice.

'If any Person within these seven Years past has taken it without Success, the Author desires that Person to advertise the same, provided he was not afflicted with other Disorders at the same time; and if all have been Cured who have taken it, Is it not a Specific worthy of the publick Cognizance.'

The advertisement noted that each twelve penny box, containing usually enough to cure three or four Persons, and sometimes as many more, with printed Directions to prevent Counterfeits, is sealed with the Author's own Butt, and the words, The Rev. Mr. Clendon, and adding: 'These Pills (which never lose their Virtue, if kept dry) are appointed by the Author to be sold at the Printing-Office in Canterbury. They are also sold by retail at Mrs. Drayson's, shop keeper in Faversham.

BRING AWAY WORMS FROM YOUNG AND OLD

The late 1740s also sees the first promotions in the *Kentish Weekly Post* or *Canterbury Journal* (illustrated courtesy of the British Newspaper Archive) for The Famous Purging SUGAR PILLS. The advertisement continues with: 'So Universally Known and Esteemed, and Daily used In Numbers of Families with great Success, for carrying off by Purging all Scorberick and foul Humours: They bring away WORMS Alive from old or Young People, purge them from the Body and prevent Worms breeding in it, by cleansing the Stomach and Bowels of the putrid Flegm which breeds in them. Children, who have generally an Aversion to the taking of bitter Potions, may without the usual Trouble, have this Physick given unto them; and many Hundreds Young and Old, have since their first Invention, found the Benefit thereof: And should a particular Account be given of all that have been Cured of Worms and other Distempers by theses PILLS, it would fill many Sheets.'

To aid diagnosis the advertisement continues with: 'The Signs of having Worms are, a stinking Breath, troublesome Sleep, frightful Dreams, grinding the Teeth, picking the Nose, hollow Eyes, a dry Cough, Vomiting, Thirstiness, swelled Belly, and many times the Belly grows less for want of that Nourishment which Worms consume ; the Children have a Weakness in their Joints, are Rickety,

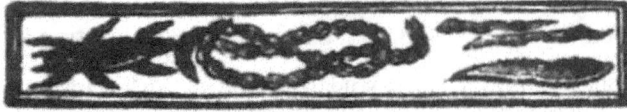

The Famous Purging SUGAR PILLS.

SO Univerfally Known and Efteemed, and Daily ufed In Numbers of Families with great Succefs, for carrying off by Purging all fcorbutick and foul Humours : They bring away WORMS Alive from Old or Young People, purge them from the Body, and prevent Worms breeding in it, by cleanfing the Stomach and Bowels of the putrid Flegm which breeds them. Children, who have generally an Averfion to the taking of bitter Portions, may without the ufual Trouble, have this Phyfick given unto them ; and many Hundreds Young and Old, have, fince their firft Invention, found the Benefit thereof: And fhould a particular Account be given of all that have been Cured of Worms and other Diftempers by thefe PILLS, it would fill many Sheets.

The Signs of having Worms are, a finking Breath, troublefome Sleep, frightful Dreams, grinding the Teeth, picking the Nofe, hollow Eyes, a dry Cough, Vomiting, Thirftinefs, fwell'd Belly, and many times the Belly grows lefs for want of that Nourifhment which Worms confume ; the Children have a Weaknefs in their Joints, are Ricketty, very Drowfie, puffed up with Wind and Vapours, that fly from the Stomach to the Brain like the Steem of a Pot, and caufe a Mift before the Eyes, almoft to Blindnefs.

And as for AGUES and FEVERS, thefe SUGAR-PILLS are now a fo well known prefent Cure, (if taken five or fix Hours before the coming of the Fit) that lately, when thofe Diftempers were fo fatal throughout the Kingdom, they Cured thofe immediately who took them. when fometimes Two at a time lay dead in thefe Families who did not take them.

Price One Shilling the Box, with full Directions for their Ufe.

Appointed to be Sold at the Printing Office in Canterbury, and at no other Place in that City and Neighbourhood.

And at the fame Place may be had,

2. The very Beft *Queen of Hungary's Water*, at 6d. or s d a Bottle.

very Drowsie, puffed up with Wind and Vapours, that fly from the Stomach to the Brain like the Steam of a Pot, and cause Mist before the Eyes, almost to Blindness.

'And as for AGUES and FEVERS, these SUGAR-PILLS are now a so well known present Cure, (if taken five or six Hours before the coming of the Fit) that lately, when those Distempers were so fatal throughout the Kingdom, they Cured those immediately who took them, when sometimes Two at a time lay dead in Families who did not take them.'

The Sugar Pills were priced at one shilling a box, including full directions for their use. Again sold at the Printing Office in Canterbury and at no other place in the City or Neighbourhood.

UNREGULATED CLAIMS AND SUCCESSES

What is interesting in nearly all the advertising and promotion of these early 1700s medications is that they mostly carry a King's Patent, Patent, Seal or dedicated logo as a sign of authenticity, and to hopefully deter attempts at counterfeiting. Many of them went on to become successful brand-name best seller remedies over many decades, both in Great Britain and then also in America.

The other noticeable factor is that they all carried unregulated claims about their efficacy and success in treating patients – even to the extent of saying that the medication cured 'All known ills.' A number also printed testimonials as to their efficacy. Sales and marketing gimmicks were also widely used – free pamphlets on treating illnesses, special offers and bargain packs, no cure, no money, special bottle shapes. Many of the marketing and publicity claims have long-since been disallowed under consumer or drug regulations. Medicine in the early, even later, 1700s was still very much in the early stages of their development. Many diseases, including dysentery, smallpox, chicken pox, measles and the plague were rampant and often proved to be fatal; hospitals were not always safe and treatment and care was poor; medicinal treatment at this time was largely non-existent or ineffectual, and medications that were now starting to appear on the market, and that promised cures, offered hope to those whose families were afflicted. Even at this time, these new medications were not cheap. At two shilling for a box of pills in 1750, it is the equivalent of around £12 today.

The newspapers of the time were undoubtedly vital to not only providing the publicity for these new quack medications, but in many cases (as frequently mentioned above) also the sales outlets for them, and even for delivery of the medications. Indeed, it has been said that without carrying these new patent and quack medicine advertisements, and the subsequent medication sales, many of the early newspapers would most likely have become bankrupt and ceased trading, nor would many of the medications' creators and/or purveyors become wealthy citizens.

But would all this continue into the second half of the 1700s and through the 1800s? Would medications and treatments change? The following chapters will look at how the history of illnesses, treatment and medication in Kent continued to evolve.

DEVELOPMENT OF MEDICATIONS IN THE LATE 1700s

While many of the early patent, proprietary and quack medications, such as Dr. John Hooper's Female Pills, and the Rev Clendon's Fever Pill or Powder, Daffy's Elixir and Dr. Bateman's Drops, continued selling well through the 1700 and well into the 1800s, their success soon spurred a number of new physicians, alchemists and chemists to look at these successes and work to develop and/or market their own medications, as well as bringing forth charlatans that started creating all kinds of counterfeit products that then also ended-up appearing in the newspapers.

By the early 1780s, the *Kentish Weekly Post* or *Canterbury Journal*, and now also the *Kentish Gazette*, were already carrying various new advertisements for aperient pills (more commonly known today as laxatives), chilblain remedies, treatments for complaints of virgins, for smelling salts, cures for gravel and stones, with many claiming extraordinary treatment efficacy in, say, the curing of rheumatism and lumbago, with marketing messages that were becoming even more outrageous, including 'it is the very best application for Chilblains and Chaps' or 'that it will cure every disorder that the human frame is incident to' or 'infinitely superior to every other' and what about 'Gravel and stones are complaints which every person is liable to, as the air we breathe and the element we drink, are impregnated with particles which are foundation for every other disorder?'

Counterfeiting, copying or imitating of medications was also become an increasing problem during the later decades of the 1700s, with proprietors adding to their sales messages statements such as 'so numerous are the counterfeits and imitations in all parts of the town and country, that it has become absolutely necessary to request that all Purchasers will particularly attend to caution, by which means they will prevent frauds, and may be sure to avail themselves of the virtues of the genuine preparation.' Messages provided with medication now included instructions for use; lists of ingredients; guarantees of efficacy; patent seals; and sometimes the purveyor's signature, while uniquely-shaped bottles or boxes also found favour with some purveyors.

UNIVERSALLY ACKNOWLEDGED AS THE BEST

In December 1781, the *Kentish Gazette* carried its first advertisement for a new medication, Dr. STEER's OPODELDOC which claimed to be the best application for Chilblains and Chaps in the hands and feet, stating that 'Its superior efficacy in the cure of bruises, sprains, the lumbago, and other rheumatic complaints, had been proved in innumerable cases. It will frequently afford immediate relief in pains of the face and rheumatism of the head, by rubbing of it on the pain externally, and by putting into the ear a bit of cotton dipped in a little of the Opodeldoc dissolved in the same manner, it will often cure the ear tooth-ach.'

Dr. Steer's Opodeldoc appears to have been a reputable liniment and was made from soap, camphor, rosemary oil, spirit of wine and, sometimes, including spirit of ammonia. Having said that, it was a liniment that could also be easily mixed at home or by any chemist or alchemist. Dr Steer claimed to be the son of the original inventor.

An interesting footnote in the Opodeldoc advertisements noted that the medication was 'of infinite service in hot climates for treating the bites of venomous insects.' Opodeldoc was later successfully imported to the U.S. over many years.

The Opodeldoc medication was sold by the Proprietor, H Steers at his warehouse below Northumberland House, Charing Cross, and (by appointment) by F. Newbery, the Corner of St. Paul's Church Yard, London, in Bottles Priced at 2s. 6d or !s. 6d. each. Likewise sold in Kent by Simmons and Kirby, Canterbury; T. Fisher, Rochester: W. Gillman, Chatham; Mrs. Senior, Sittingborn; J. Sharpe, Deal; R. Emmerson, Sandwich; and may be had carriage free of the Newsmen. Good Allowance made to Country Dealers, who are desired to apply to Mr. Newbery only, as above.

At about the same time as Opodeldoc arrived in Kent, came the first Kent newspaper promotion for Dalby's Carminative medication. This appeared as follows:

FOR DISORDERS OF THE BOWELS, &cc. DALBY's CARMINATIVE. This Medicine, which is founded on just Medical Principles, has been long established as a most safe, and effectual Remedy, generally affording immediate Relief, in the Wind, Cholics, Convulsions, Purgings, and all those fatal Disorders in the Bowels of Infants, which cry off for a great number under the Age of Two Years. It is also equally efficacious in Gouty Pains in the Intestines, in Fluxes, and the Cholicky Complaints of grown Persons, so useful at this season the Year.

It is prepared by the Inventor, J. Dalby, Apothecary, and sold wholesale and Retail only, by Francis Newbery, Junior, removed to his New Medicinal Warehouse, No, 45, the East End of St.

Paul's, on the Coach Way, five doors from Cheapside London, Price is 6d. a Bottle.

Sold also by Simmons and Kirkby, Canterbury; T. Fisher, Rochester; W, Gillman, Chatham; J. Sharp, Deal; F. Cocking, Sandwich; Mrs Crux, Ramsgate; and J. Constable, Romney ; and may be had (carriage free) of the Newsman.

Dalby's Carminative was said to be one of the most widely used patent medicines given to babies and children at the end of the 1700s and into the 1800s, and was to become another English medication that was a hit in North America. However, its main active ingredient was opium, giving rise to stories of nurses overdosing babies in their care to keep them quiet. Joseph Dalby was a surgeon and apothecary in London from around 1770.

In the same issue of the newspaper there was also another advertisement under the main heading of GRAVEL and STONE; Stoppage of Urine; Complaints in the Back, Kidneys, and Bladder, &c. effectually cured; and lost Appetite restored. This heading was followed by several paragraphs of copy to describe the nature and use of HICKMAN'S Original Pills as a cure, noting as follows:

'The Gravel and Stone are complaints which every person is liable to, as the air we breathe and the element we drink, are impregnated with particles which are foundation for every other disorder. HICKMAN'S original PILLS, compos'd of the most innocent ingredients, are of singular efficacy in not only strengthening the vessels containing the urine, but destroying the petrifying qualities without confinement.'

It then went on to add that 'After a private practice of many years, these Pills are now publicly offered to the afflicted. — To advance that they will cure every disorder which the human frame is incident to, would be adopting the stile of a QUACK — they are therefore recommended as salutary for a cure of the above complaints only, by a safe and gentle operation, without the least painful sensation They are made up in oval boxes, labelled HICKMAN's original PILLS, for the effectual cure of the Gravel and Stone, &c, for Three Shillings per Box, directions included, sealed W. J. H. with the motto Amicis prodeffe Nemine Nocere — Also signed W. J. H on the inside of the cover.'

Hickman's Pills were sold by appointment of the proprietor, wholesale and retail in London, only by M. and H. Wray, Birch Lane, London, but now also readily Sold retail throughout Kent by Simmons and Kirkby, Canterbury; Mr. Pike, Ashford; Mr. Reeve, Margate; Mr.Fisher, Rochester; Mr. Gillman, Chatham Mr. Sharp. Deal; Mrs. Walker, Maidstone; Mr. Hall, Tenterden; Mr. Clifford, Cranbrook; Mr. Neave, Hythe; Mr. Walker, Faversham; Mr. Grover, Malling; and at every principal Town in England. N.B. The proprietor is unavoidably obliged to raise the price of the Pills to Three Shillings per box, on account of the very great advance on medicine.

SUPERIOR EFFICACY AS A PURGATIVE

Another medication that first appears in Kent newspapers from the early 1780s is again for APERIENT PILLS, For Costiveness, Indigestion, Cholic, Jaundice, Worms, and other Complaints of the Stomach and Bowels.

The advertisement stated that MR. WILLIAMS, Apothecary, No.

46, Charing-cross, is induced to offer the Public his very easy and safe opening medicine, from his long experience in various cases of its superior efficacy as a purgative, devoid of the heating effects of aloctics, &c. In the complaints enumerated as above, these Pills are deserving great confidence; and for those who suffer from habitual costiveness they are particularly eligible. They readily and most properly remove bile, and in sickness of stomach there-from, or from liquor, indigestion, and in the bilious head-ach, may be taken with great advantage. In short, in all complaints, where a laxative is necessary, (whether fever be present or not) the Aperient Pills will constantly afford every aid to expected from Scot's Pills, electuaries in the shops, or similar purgatives, without the their unpleasant subsequent effects.

Aperient Pills were sold by appointment of T. Williams, the Proprietor, by W. Bacon, at his Royal Patent Genuine Medicinal Warehouse. No. 150, Oxford Street, (opposite New Bond-street) in boxes priced 1s.6d. for three boxes, in one at 4s. and six boxes in one at 7s. 6d. stamps included.

Mr. Bacon's name is signed by him on every stamp, as a guard against fraud. Once again, the pills are made available throughout Kent and sold, by Mr. Bacon's appointment, by Simmons and Kirkby, Canterbury; Gillman, Rochester; Burgess, Ramsgate; Ledger, Dover; Long, Deal; Cocking and Son, Sandwich; Silver, Margate; Wakefield, Folkestone; Neve, Hythe; Pike, Romney; Bailey, Ashford ; Hall, Tenterden; Barnard, Sittingbourne; Merton, Milton; Coveney, Faversham; and Clout, Sevenoaks.

Another medication introduced from the early 1780s was

MONTPELIER DROPS which claimed to be 'the most sovereign remedy in the world for those troublesome exhausting colds, coughs, asthmas, and consumptions, with which many are severely troubled Night and Morning; and also for what is called HOOPING COUGH, or CHIN COUGH, in children, having cured thousands. It is so agreeable, and so few drops to a dose, that children may taken them dropped on small lumps of sugar, with pleasure without confinement.'

Also at the same time, came an advertisement for THE FAMOUS PATENT OINTMENT for the ITCH, which was claimed to effectually cure that distemper at one dressing, without the least danger: it was also claimed to cleanse the body from all spots, blotches, scurvical itchings, or breakings out whatsoever, as thousands, to their great joy, have happily experienced. It was said to be one of the safest and best remedies for the distemper even found, and was never known to fail.

The ointment also noted that it did not stain the finest linen, had a delightful smell, and made the skin extremely smooth and soft; and for its safety could be applied to a sucking child. One box, priced 1s. 6d was said to be sufficient to cure a grown person, and divided, was a cure for two children.

HELD IN HIGHEST ESTEEM BY EUROPEAN GENTRY

While Montpelier Drops were claimed to be 'the most sovereign remedy in the world' in 1780, another interesting product with extensive claims of its instantaneous relief and superiority was being launched in the *Kentish Gazette* in January 1783 under the following heading:

THE CURIOUS SMELLING-BOTTLE

Called

Le SELPOIGNANT d'ANGLETERRE

Held in the highest esteem by all the quality and gentry throughout Europe, who constantly carry it in their Pocket: and is infinitely superior to every other Kind of Salts hitherto invented and far more fragrant and refreshing than either Lavendar, Hungary, any Kind of essence, or Odoriferous Water. Its Uses. By smelling it, it gives instantaneous Relief in all Sorts of Head Aches. Sickness, Faintings, Swoonings, Tremblings, Sudden Frights, Hysteric and Hypochondrical Disorders. Oppression, and Palpitation of the Heart, Melancholy, Lowness of Spirits, Anxiety, Inquietudes, and all the whole Train of Nervous Disorders. Add to these most excellent qualities, only by opening the Stopper now and then, it gives a most pleasing and agreeable Flavour in a room, or any public Place; and by its penetrating and discutient Effluvia is a certain Preventative from the Small Pox, Measles, and every kind of Infectious Disorder.

In order to preserve the Reputation these most excellent Smelling Bottles, the Public are requested to observe, that L. J. from Dalmahoy, is engraved on each bottle. This restorative is to be had in bottles at 1l. 1s. and 10s. 6d. each, with full directions from booksellers in Kent, and of the Doctor in Suffolk Street, near Charing-cross, who may be consulted personally, or by letter, post paid. The Guinea bottles to be had only at the Doctor's.

COMPLAINTS PECULIAR TO VIRGINS, MARRIED WOMEN AND THOSE WITH VENEREAL DISEASE

By the later years of the 1780s, Dr. John Hopper's Female Pills had already been around, with great success, for well over a hundred years. It was therefore probably of no great surprise that others should come along with their own claims for curing female diseases and disorders. Some of the more notable of this time were Welch's Female Obstruction Pills and Leak's famous pill for curing venereal disease, which are both examined below.

Promoted in the *Kentish Gazette* in 1780, Leake's Pills, called PILULA SALUTARIA, in the Patent, were pronounced as a cure for Venereal Disease, the Scurvy and Rheumatism, noting that 'In fifteen days it generally cures these disorders.' The advertisement noted that 'it is an excellency of the pills to make directly to the complaining part, and enter into contest with the offending matter, which they suddenly dislodge and expel. They are declared by experience to be a preserver of health, as well as a restorer, by taking only eight single pills once or twice a year.'

Like many of the pills and potions now coming into the Kentish market, Leake's Pills were sold by Simmons and Kirkby, Canterbury, and extensively throughout the county by booksellers, grocers and other retail outlets in Kent's main towns. Sold in boxes of 2s. 6d. each, it stated that the Pills were most worthy of a place in the cabinets of masters and captains of ships, as they require no confinement nor restraint of diet of the patient, and will keep good in all climates for any length of time.

Perhaps of even more interest to the female sex and to doctors' treating them were Welch's Pills for complaints peculiar to virgins. The commercial production of these pills, justly celebrated for all female complaints, had begun in 1787 when a Catherine Kearsley and her husband, who were printers and booksellers in London, adopted a family recipe to produce Welch's Female Pills. Their advertisement for the Pills first started to appear in the *Kentish Gazette*, such as the one set-out below, from 1787 onwards, and continued to be a popular medication right up to the late 1960s, when the company finally ceased trading.

FEMALE OBSTRUCTIONS.

WELCH's PILLS.

THE Proprietor of these PILLS, being conscious of their Excellence, and above Deception, will content himself with asserting, that their Efficacy is fully established wherever they have been tried, in Complaints peculiar to VIRGINS, their Effort being to remove OBSTRUCTIONS, correct bad DIGESTION, cure GIDDINESS and create an APPETITE. They are excellent for pains in the STOMACH, Shortness of BREATH, and HEAD-ACHS. MARRIED WOMEN will materially benefited by taking them three or four Weeks after Delivery: They raise the Spirits and are great Strengtheners of Nature. They are likewise strongly recommended to the other Sex, who may have injured their Constitutions by Irregularities.

The Price of Welch's Pills was Two Shillings and Threepence per Box. They could be had, with Directions, of Mr. Kearsley, Bookseller, No. 46, Fleet-Street, opposite Fetter Lane, London. They are also, by the Proprietor's Appointment, to be had of Simmons and Kirkby,

Dr. ARNOLD's PILLS,
WHICH are univerſally known to be a ſafe, certain and expeditious remedy for the VENEREAL DISEASE, without confinement or hinderance of buſineſs, when ſalivation and all other methods would not avail. Printed directions, ſigned by Dr. Arnold, are encloſed with each box, which will enable all perſons to cure themſelves with the greateſt ſecrecy.
Prepared and ſold, wholeſale, by Dr. Arnold, at Slough, near Windſor, and retail by W. Briſtow, Canterbury, and Mr. French, Dover.

Canterbury; Hall, Margate; Burgess, Ramsgate; and Ledger, Dover.

By the middle 1790s a further treatment for Venereal Disease was being advertised in the *Kentish Weekly Post* or *Canterbury Journal*. Promoted as a universally known and safe, certain and expeditious remedy for the disease, Dr. ARNOLD'S PILLS treated Venereal Disease without confinement or hindrance of business when salivation and all other methods would not avail. The promotion noted that printed directions, signed by Dr. Arnold, were enclosed with each box, which would enable all persons to cure themselves with the greatest secrecy. They were available from Dr. Arnold, at Slough, and retailed by W. Bristow, Canterbury, and Mr. French, Dover.

MOST VALUABLE AND INFALLIBLE MEDICINES EVER OFFERED FOR WORMS

The late 1700s was a time when an even greater variety of cures for worms were appearing in the market, many claiming some quite extraordinary successes in eliminating worms in both children and adults. Two of these specific worm medications by Drs. Waite and

Kendrick are briefly set out below, and in the associated newspaper advertisement and leaflet.

The first of these two worm medications was promoted as the only pleasant Worm Medicine for Children, and was headed DR. WAITE's improved WORM MEDICINE. This medication was In the form of Gingerbread Nuts, and claimed to be esteemed, by all who have made trial of it as the most valuable and best adapted Worm Medicine for Children ever yet offered to the Public.

Independent of its superior efficacy as a Worm Medicine, Dr. Waite's noted that it has been found to answer better than any other preparation tor inoculation, as a cleanser after the Small Pox, for Scorbutic humour, and all complaints arising from a foul stomach. The sore eyes, sore ears, and scabby heads, with the other complaints that so commonly attend teething in children, are generally removed by taking a few doses.

At around the same time, Dr. KENDRICK was advertising his Famous WORM SUGAR CAKES, for killing and destroying of

Worms in the bodies of men, women and children. Said to have been used for a great many years in practice, and having been tried in most cities and market town throughout Great Britain and Ireland, has performed many wonderful cures, brought away numbers of monstrous and different kinds of worms, and having cured numbers of persons of very bad disorders and of long-standing, which many can witness.

It was claimed that the cakes were the only physic yet known in any distemper where purging is required, such as small pox, measles, black and yellow jaundice. The advertisements noted that the cakes were as pleasant as sweetmeats; they worked very gently by stool, and may be called an infallible remedy in all the above disorders.

SUBSCRIPTIONS TO THE KENT COUNTY HOSPITAL

With the ever-rising cost of today's NHS Hospitals, it is perhaps worth noting this report of the General Meeting of the Subscribers to the County Hospital, Canterbury, at their meeting at the King's Head, Canterbury, on the 8th September, 1792, which appeared in the *Kentish Gazette* in November 1792.

This report stated that the annual subscriptions, which amounted only to 200 pounds, were not adequate to the experience of opening the Hospital for the reception of patients. It noted that 'by examining the accounts of other hospitals, it appeared that the full number of fifty patients could not be maintained for less than 700 pounds a year, and that an establishment for twenty-five would cost between 400 and 500 pounds.'

The aim of the newspaper message was to impress these facts on the public; that an establishment of this kind must, in every respect, be more particularly beneficial to Canterbury and its neighbourhood. It therefore submitted to the Clergy and Churchwardens, assisted by two or three respectable inhabitants, to solicit annual subscriptions of such persons, whom they think may be able to contribute.

PILLS FOR MEN'S HEALTH AND LONGEVITY

It was just a couple of years after the County Hospital was established that a new medication to preserve health and prolong life, and hopefully keep people away from hospital, was being advertised in the *Kentish Weekly Post* or *Canterbury Journal*. This was for Dr. JAMES's ANALEPTIC PILLS which stated in its promotion that 'nothing is so necessary as an attention to those slight indispositions to which all men are subject, and which by being considered as trifling, are too often disregarded, till by neglect they take deep root in the constitution, and become of serious and sometimes of fatal consequence.'

The advertisement continued by adding 'These complaints, whether the cause of them be a cold, excess of eating or drinking, fatigue of body or mind, a too active or too sedentary life, a gouty or billious disposition, &c, are generally discovered by some obstructions in the minute vessels, or some defect in the natural secretions of the body.'

It was as a remedy for these evils that the celebrated inventor of the Fever Powder, Dr. James, had composed his ANALEPTIC PILLS, and exhibited in himself a memorable instance of their efficacy; for by constant use of them, through a free liver, he had attained the age of seventy five. It continued to add that 'they were also an admirable remedy for rheumatic fever, for headache, and for those complaints for which the female sex are peculiarly subject.' The pills were priced at 4s. 6d. for a box and sold by W. Bristow, Canterbury, and his agents.

More or less at the same time as the Analeptic Pills were being advertised, another medication that claimed to preserve health and extend the duration of life to old age in comfort, was appearing in the *Kentish Gazette*. This was for Dr. SMITH's GOLDEN PURIFYING PILLS, an entirely vegetable composition with unequalled efficacy and safety. These pills claimed to give relief in all cases of Billious, Bowel, and Liver complaints, Piles, Gravel, Sick Head Ach, after intemperance in drinking, in all Female Complaints, to assist digestion, create an appetite, and are deserving of those that take little or no exercise. It was also noted that they were also beneficial previous to sea bathing, and were invaluable on a voyage.

FIRST EXPERIMENTS WITH VACCINES

It was in 1796 that doctor and scientist Edward Jenner, a country doctor in Gloucestershire, started the development of a vaccine that would prevent people from catching smallpox, a deadly disease that killed more children each year in Great Britain than any other disease, and also killed thousands of adults. Even if they survived they would be left with scars that frequently left them isolated in society.

Jenner noticed that milkmaids who caught the mild cowpox disease did not go on to catch smallpox. He tested his observations with a series of experiments, recording his findings and, in 1798, published a book describing how to prevent people from catching smallpox by injecting them with cowpox. He named his treatment vaccination, after vacca the Latin name for cow.

Although vaccination proved to be successful, some doctors opposed it, the Church didn't like the concept of using a disease from cows in humans, and the Royal Society refused to publish his ideas and developments.

SPEEDY REMOVAL AND RADICAL CURE OF A CERTAIN SECRET DISORDER

Towards the very end of the 1700s a new medication is announced for curing those afflicted with that dreadful complaint for which THE SYPHILITIC MEZEREON PILLS 'would easily cure themselves with the greatest safety, secrecy, and expedition, without restraint of diet, hindrance of business, or any mercurial preparation whatsoever.' Sealed up with plain directions and specific instructions, it said that the lives of thousands may be rendered comfortable, and preserved from the horrible ravages which are daily made by that cruel insidious and malignant disease.

The Mezereon Pills were prepared by Dr. Paterson, Little Tower Street, London, and sold at 5s. 5d. throughout Kent by appointed booksellers and retailers. It was noted that anyone desiring the Doctor's advice could only do so by sending a post paid letter.

One final announcement in the late 1700 was for JACKSON's ORIGINAL OINTMENT for infallibly curing the ITCH with just two rubbings. In an advertisement in the *Kentish Weekly Post* or *Canterbury Journal* in September 1797, it wrote that the medication 'did not contain the least particle of mercury, or any other pernicious ingredient, and could be used with safety by women with child, and newly-born infants, and is not disagreeable in flavour.'

This advertisement was coupled with a brief follow-on advert for Barclay's ASTHMATIC CANDY, an effective remedy for asthmatic coughs and shortness of breath, windy complaints, and weakness of the stomach.

So completes the list of medications that were announced and promoted in Kent during the later years of the 1700s. A continuation of wild claims and curative powers for medications that sold in their thousands in Kent, through Great Britain and in the USA.

MEDICINE AND TREATMENTS MOVE INTO THE 19TH CENTURY

Medicine, surgery, operations and healthcare all started to undergo quite important and significant changes from the early and middle years of the 1800s, with major advances in the treatment of infections, better prevention of disease, the ongoing development of vaccines and how to use them, and experimentations by surgeons to find an effective anaesthetic for use in surgical operations, as well as to ease the pain that women suffered during childbirth.

Medical students in Georgian London from the mid-1700s had already undertaken teaching that included dissection of bodies – some dug up from graves, some donated to scientific research, some obtained from workhouse and infirmaries, and some, in Kent, simply purchasing bodies from the quite numerous hangings at Penenden Heath, near Maidstone. Indeed, records from the passing of the Anatomy Bill in 1832, indicate that the bodies of nearly six thousand honest poor persons who were inmates of charitable institutions, had been given over for dissection, together with a near two thousand convicted and hanged felons bodies.

An unexpected consequence of bodies being obtained for dissection and anatomical research in the 1840s, can be ascertained from a report in the *Kentish Gazette*, 6th February 1844, which stated: 'Our attention has not un-frequently been drawn to the subject of Human Anatomy, as practised in the Medical and Surgical Schools of the present day. The principal in force in these institutions of the sale of limbs at a large percentage profit (said to be from 1,000 to 2,000 per cent), is almost too horrible for belief, were it not asserted by the testimony of persons whose credit is unimpeachable.

Advertisement from the Maidstone and South Eastern Gazette in 1848, by kind permission of the British Newspaper Archive.

Surely a remedy may be suggested by the Legislature.'

A subsequent consequence of this proposal was that in 1844 a petition to Parliament, numerously signed by the inhabitants of Canterbury, in the County of Kent, was seeking to obtain justice for the poor and destitute, asking for 'a Committee to be appointed, to institute an impartial, searching, and open enquiry into the operation of the Anatomy Act – including the lucrative trade in bodies and body parts,' largely obtained from workhouses and infirmaries. This would be where live-in nurses at that time received no more than £20 per annum, plus rations (See advertisement).

Nevertheless, by the mid-1800s, knowledge of how the body worked that had been ascertained by medical students was greater than ever, all massively contributing to modern medicine and surgery. Indeed medical schools were so popular in the late Georgian period that the natural consequence was a great glut of medical students during the 1840s.

At around the same time, research by organic chemists and scientists in the 1800s was also leading to work on the isolation of the specific active ingredients found in medicinal plants, with the new and emerging drug companies, such as Smith, Kline & French, and Beecham's (which went on to become part of Glaxo SmithKline), beginning to replicate cheaper synthetic versions of these active ingredients as well as to create their own drug solutions.

Interestingly, Thomas Beecham's background was as a chemist who had earlier worked as a shepherd boy, creating various herbal remedy concoctions to tend his livestock as a sideline, later becoming a travelling salesman and full-time producer and peddler of pills. His first product was Beecham's Pills, a laxative, in 1842. Moving to the mill towns in the North West of England, he sold his pills from a market stall, opening his first

A Wonderful Medicine,

BEECHAM'S PILLS

For Bilious and Nervous Disorders, such as Wind and Pain in the Stomach, Sick Headache, Giddiness, Fulness and Swelling after meals, Dizziness and Drowsiness, Cold Chills, Flushings of Heat, Loss of Appetite, Shortness of Breath, Costiveness, Blotches on the Skin, Disturbed Sleep, Frightful Dreams, and all Nervous and Trembling Sensations, &c. **THE FIRST DOSE WILL GIVE RELIEF IN TWENTY MINUTES.** This is no fiction. Every sufferer is earnestly invited to try one Box of these Pills, and **they will be acknowledged to be**

WORTH A GUINEA A BOX.

BEECHAM'S PILLS taken as directed, will quickly restore Females to complete health. They promptly remove any obstruction or irregularity of the system. For a

Weak Stomach,

Impaired Digestion,

Disordered Liver,

they act like magic—a few doses will work wonders upon the Vital Organs; Strengthening the muscular System, restoring the long-lost Complexion, bringing back the keen edge of appetite, and arousing with the Rosebud of Health the whole physical energy of the human frame. These are "facts" admitted by thousands, in all classes of society, and one of the best guarantees to the Nervous and Debilitated is that *BEECHAM'S PILLS have the Largest Sale of any Patent Medicine In the World.*

Beecham's Pills have been before the public for half a century, and are the popular English family medicine. No testimonials are published, as Beecham's Pills

RECOMMEND THEMSELVES.

Prepared only by

THOMAS BEECHAM, ST. HELENS, LANCS.

Sold everywhere in Boxes 1/1½ & 2/9 each

shop in Wigan in 1847, and his first factory in 1849 for the rapid production of patent medicines.

Beecham's Pills comprised of aloes, ginger and soap and were deemed more palatable than many of the other traditional home remedies regularly advertised in English and Kent newspapers (Shown as illustrated from the *Canterbury Journal*) throughout the late 1800s and 1900s, such as Dr. John Armstrong's Anti-bilious Liver Pills.

Beecham's Pills claimed to cure bilious and nervous disorders, more commonly described today as indigestion and constipation, and were successfully produced continuously from 1842 right up until 1998, aided by relentless advertising. They later claimed to have the largest sale of any patent medicine in the world, with Beecham's Pills acting like "MAGIC," with a few doses working wonders on the most important organs in the human machine.

Regularly advertised alongside Beecham's Pills were BEECHAM'S MAGIC COUGH PILLS, a remedy for coughs in general, asthma, bronchial affections, hoarseness, shortness of breath, tightness and oppression of the chest, noting that any person giving the pills a trial will find the most violent cough being removed in a short time.

With so many wild claims for medicines and their efficacy in the later years of the 1800s, it was not unsurprising that moves were soon being made to regulate the claims that were being made on the labels of medicine bottles and boxes and their accompanying leaflets, and for proprietors and drug manufacturers being required to prove the safety and efficacy of the drugs being sold.

EXTENSIVE USE OF TESTIMONIALS IN ADVERTISING

It was not just medicines and pills that claimed all kinds of successes; by the second half of the 1800s, advertising for all kinds of treatments were appearing in Kent newspapers, such as the one shown on page 58 from the *Maidstone Journal* and *Kentish Advertiser* in December 1867, by Mrs. Upton, of Mount Pleasant Villa, Maidstone, an experienced Chiropodist of twenty-four years practice, and an 'Anatomical Professor of the Pathology of the Human Foot.'

As can be seen (overleaf), the advertisement carries numerous Testimonials from satisfied customers all around Kent who had been operated on by Mrs. Upton to remove corns and treat in-growing toe-nails successfully, without pain or any loss of blood, so giving great relief from pain. Mrs. Upton also provided a lotion for weak ankles, damp feet, chilblains, &c. in bottles at 1s., 2s., or 5s. each. Judging by the size of the advertisement she appears to have been very successful in her business, travelling all over Kent and even providing home visits at no extra charge.

Also during the late 1800s and early 1900s came the development of modern antibiotics and antiseptics that can kill or inhibit the growth of bacteria to reduce the death rate in surgical operations, as well as chemicals that could be selectively used to kill bacteria.

Prior to these developments, infections were treated with various moulds and plant extracts, although it was not known that the infections were actually caused by bacteria. All these area are reviewed in this and other chapters in the book.

MAIDSTONE AND KENTISH JOURNAL, DEC. 9. 1867.

Notices.

MRS. UPTON,
MOUNT PLEASANT VILLA, NEAR THE CEMETERY, MAIDSTONE.
AN EXPERIENCED CHIROPODIST OF TWENTY-FOUR YEARS' PRACTICE.
Anatomical Professor of the Pathology of the Human Foot.

A great boon is now offered to sufferers, as the most troublesome corns, both hard and soft, are removed either from children or adults on an entirely new system, without the slightest pain whatever, thereby enabling the patient to walk with the greatest ease and comfort.

CHARGE MODERATE.

Families waited on at their own residence without extra charge.

Attendance on THURSDAYS, from 11 a.m. till 6 p.m., at E. Vinson's, Chemist, 6 & 9, Middle-row, High-street, Maidstone.

Lotion for weak ankles, damp feet, chilblains, &c., in bottles 1s., 2s., or 5s. each. Corn salve, 1s. per box.

TESTIMONIALS.

Ramsgate, August 24th, 1867.
Mrs. Upton has operated on my corns very judiciously and effectively.
JOSEPH SEATON, M.D., Sunbury.

I hereby certify that Mrs. Upton has operated on my corns and toenails successfully, and has afforded me great relief.
J. HUGHES MURTAGH, M.D.
East Cliff House, Ramsgate, and London.

5, Nelson Place, Broadstairs, August 2nd, 1867.
Mrs. Upton has extracted three corns from my feet without causing pain, and the relief I feel is most satisfactory.
GEORGE CLARKE.

2, Harbour-street, Ramsgate, August 3rd, 1867.
I feel great pleasure in stating that Mrs. Upton has removed several corns from my feet without causing any pain, thereby giving me immense relief.
H. A. JONES.

East Cliff House, Ramsgate, August 21st, 1867.
I have great pleasure in stating that Mrs. Upton has entirely cured me of a most painful corn, without the least pain or annoyance.
DONALD HADFIELD SMITH.

Ramsgate, August 26th, 1867.
Mrs. Upton has extracted three very painful corns from the feet of my wife, giving her perfect ease.
EDWIN PERRY, Royal Albert Bazaar.

Elm House, Wrexham, Feb. 2nd, 1867.
I hereby certify that Mrs. Upton has removed three corns from my feet, without the slightest pain, and the relief I have since experienced is most satisfactory.
ALFRED JOHN SPENCER.

King-street, Ramsgate, July 23rd, 1867.
My corns have been taken out by Mrs. Upton quite successfully and free from pain.
GEORGE CHAPMAN.

Compton-street, Brunswick-square, March 2nd, 1867.
Madam,—It affords me much pleasure in stating that since the extraction of my corns by you, I have been perfectly free from pain. I can strongly recommend your admirable system to the public.
Yours respectfully,
F. R. MILLS.

I, Robert Hamilton, of St. Dunstan's, Canterbury, hereby certify that Mrs. Upton has removed 2 corns from between my toes which had given me great pain, and since their removal, I can walk with ease and comfort.
September 28th, 1867.

6, Gilling-place, Ramsgate, August 29th, 1867.
Mrs. Upton has extracted nine corns very satisfactorily, and without giving the least pain.
HENRY HUDSON.

Sevenoaks, February 11th, 1867.
I beg to state that in December last Mrs. Upton removed a troublesome corn from the centre of a bunion on my foot without pain or loss of blood. I can now wear my boot without the slightest inconvenience.
THOMAS TAYLOR.

Medway Terrace, Maidstone, February 20th, 1867.
Madam,—I authorize you to make the public for the benefit of those suffering from corns. In 1866 Mrs. Upton extracted a very painful soft corn from my wife's foot, which had troubled her for many years, and since that time I am thankful to say, she has felt nothing whatever of it.
CHARLES ANDERSON.

14, Ozenden-street, Dover, July 3rd, 1867.
I feel much pleasure in testifying to the great benefit derived by my son from the treatment he has received from Mrs. Upton, for a corn on the sole of his foot, and likewise for a broken chilblain, from both of which he had been suffering several months, and had not been able to walk.
CAPT. WM. SHAW,
Commanding S.S. "Pioneer."

19, Harbour Street, Ramsgate, July 9th, 1867.
Mrs. Upton has removed several corns from my feet without causing any pain or loss of blood.
W. R. WORGER.

10, Liverpool Place, Ramsgate, July 10th, 1867.
Mrs. Upton has removed a corn of long standing from my toe without pain or loss of blood. I can now walk with perfect ease and comfort, which hitherto was a misery.
JOHN BEAR.

Eaton Lodge, Stoke Newington, and 124, High-street, Ramsgate.
I have a great deal of pleasure in stating that Mrs. Upton has removed four corns of mine, which had previously caused me a great amount of suffering. I can safely recommend her novel and successful mode of treatment.
CECIL H. T. PRICE.

July 18th, 1867.

Southwood, St. Lawrence, July 15, 1867.
Mrs. Upton has most operated on my feet, and I shall be happy to state to any one personally, or by letter, the relief I have experienced. The corns were extracted without pain.
W. TAPSELL.

Albion House, High-street, Ramsgate.
I have great pleasure in confirming the foregoing and other testimonials Mrs. Upton has, she having extracted four corns from my feet in a most successful manner.
July 23rd, 1867.
JOHN SHAW.

43, Lerrimore-square, London, August 31st, 1867.
I have satisfaction in stating that Mrs. Upton has operated most skilfully and successfully on my in-grown toe-nails, and I feel quite relieved.
T. HORYAN.

East Cliff House, Ramsgate, September 6th, 1867.
I am happy to say I am again relieved from a most troublesome corn, and I will, I am sure, ever feel grateful to Mrs. Upton for the care and skill she used in extracting it.
DONALD HADFIELD SMITH.

Mrs. Upton has operated on my corns very successfully.
JOHN MAYO.

31, Paragon, Ramsgate, September 16th, 1867.
Parade, Canterbury, Sept. 28th, 1847.
I hereby certify that Mrs. Upton has operated on my wife's corns with success, and has given her great relief.
H. T. FORKMAN.

14, Dover-street, Canterbury, Oct. 19th, 1867.
I hereby certify that Mrs. Upton has operated on my corn with success and without pain, and has afforded me instant relief.
THOMAS MARSH.

Canterbury, Oct. 21st, 1867.
Leonard Woodruff has received great relief by Mrs. Upton.

12, High-street, Canterbury, Oct. 22nd, 1867.
I beg to certify that Mrs. Upton has extracted several very troublesome corns from my wife's feet, which she had been suffering from for some time, and she has found great relief and comfort by their removal.
W. CHIPPERFIELD.

43, Upper Stone-street, Maidstone, January, 1867.
Madam,—I have much pleasure in stating the conversation my assistant had from you for chilblains has acted marvellously. Some of her fingers were opened almost to the bones. The first application healed them over, and in a few days they were quite well.
Yours obediently,
E. BUTTON.

A Number of Testimonials can be seen on application.

Extract from *The Thanet Advertiser*, of July 20th, 1867.

"Mrs. Upton's important discovery of a preparation for numbing the nerves, thereby rendering corn extraction a painless operation, is at once so simple and efficacious that every one recommends it."

From *Kent Coast Times*, July 25th, 1867.

"The greatest value of Mrs. Upton's system of extraction lays in the discovery by her of a certain anaesthetic or pain-destroying substance, by the use of which she is able entirely to remove all sense of pain in the nerves during the period required for the extraction of the corn."

From *The Kentish Standard*, September 28th, 1867.

"Mrs. Upton's system of extracting corns by an entirely painless operation, attended by a clever process of benumbing the part affected is spoken very highly of."

From *The Kentish Gazette*, October 8th, 1867.

"We have heard of several very successful cures having been effected by Mrs. Upton, who has achieved considerable success as a chiropodist, and would advise those who desire comfort, to apply to this lady at once."

From *The Kent Herald*, October 10th, 1867.

"Mrs. Upton, now making a stay in Canterbury, should be visited by all who suffer from corns or bunions. The excellent *bona fide* testimonials which she exhibits should induce confidence in her ability to do that which she professes—the giving relief from those most painful excrescences; and that by a process which involves no suffering during the operation, a most important thing."

THE SEARCH FOR A WONDER DRUG FOR PAIN MEDICATION IN THE 1800S

It was around 1804 that a young German apothecary's assistant (and later an outstanding pharmacist) named F.W.A. Sertürner, successfully isolated crystalline morphine contained in dried poppy resin as the active analgesic principle of opium. He utilized acetic acid to convert the basic drug to a water-soluble form which he then converted to salts. With few alternative painkillers at this time, opium soon came to be regarded as something of a medical panacea.

Mixing a tincture of opium with alcohol, under the name of

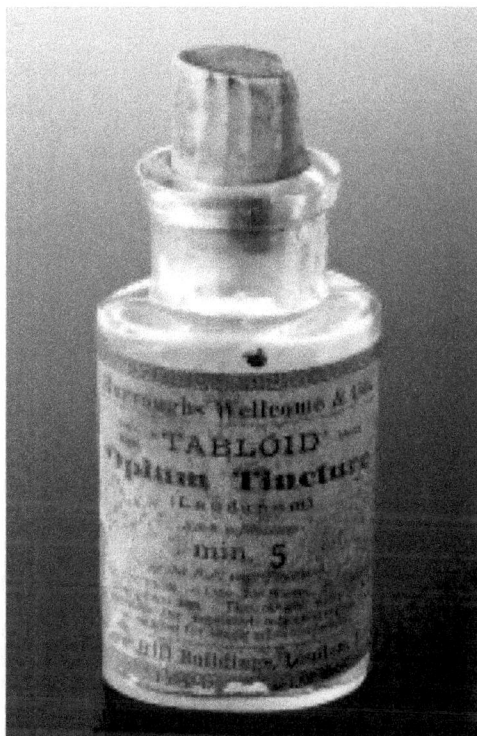

Old archive picture of an empty bottle of opium tincture or laudanum.

laudanum, had already been developed in the late 1700s and was undoubtedly already considered as a wonder drug in the late eighteen and early nineteenth centuries. Reddish-brown in colour and extremely bitter, laudanum principally contained opium alkaloids, including morphine and codeine, and was used to treat a variety of conditions. However, its primary use was as a pain medication and cough suppressant, which was usually inserted between the cheeks and gums. It was also applied under the tongue.

Opium tincture or laudanum became even more widely used in

the 19th century and was sold by barbers, tobacconists, grocers, pharmacists and stationers, as an over-the-counter pain killer or sleeping aid. It was prescribed for all kinds of ailments, from persistent coughs, belly pain, rheumatism, gout, diarrhea (also spelt diarrhoea), gripes, headache – and 'women's troubles' (probably accounting for high rates of addiction amongst women).

Cheaper than alcohol, laudanum was affordable by pretty-well all levels of 19th society. However, it was also highly addictive, leading (as already mentioned) to many of its users, particularly women, forming a drug addiction. This was especially so during Victorian times.

During the 1800s, even from the late Georgian and then the early Victorian periods, drug taking included not only alcohol and opium tinctures, but cannabis and cocao (a powerful antioxidant claimed to have anti-cancer, blood sugar regulation, heart health and immune health properties) as well.

The subsequent invention of the hypodermic needle in the middle 1800s also led to the injection of drugs containing morphine and heroin. It was not until the 1860s that laudanum and other opiates were only allowed to be sold by registered chemists in England, and additionally had to be labelled as a 'poison.'

INJECTION OF MEDICATIONS AND DRUGS TO SAVE THOUSANDS OF LIVES

As mentioned above, the invention and use of hollow stainless steel needles for injecting medications into human bodies dates from the middle 1800s. It was this invention that eventually allowed millions of people worldwide to be vaccinated. Developed by Scottish physician, Alexander Wood and French surgeon Charles Gabriel Pravaz, the first glass hypodermic syringes enabled doctors to assess a dosage by looking at the amount of liquid inside the glass. They were first used to inject morphine as a painkiller.

In the previous chapter mention had been made of Edward Jenner's discovery in 1796 of a vaccine against smallpox, a killer disease in both children) and adults in the 1700s. Jenner's vaccination was to rapidly became the means of preventing smallpox worldwide – even becoming mandatory in

An early Illustration showing a child being vaccinated during a smallpox epidemic. Courtesy of Chronicle/Alamy Stock Photo

some countries. Even as late as 1828 some 6389 infants under two years of age are recorded as dying in the City of London, and a further 2326 between the ages of two and five.

However, according to the Annual report of the National Vaccine Establishment, 1830, more than 10,000 of the poor in London and its neighbourhood had been vaccinated during that year. It also noted that there had been no increase in the cases of smallpox after vaccination.

Now combined with Wood's invention of the hypodermic needle, a new era of successfully treating and preventing infectious diseases had become available, launching a revolution in global health care, and probably providing the single most life-saving innovation in the long history of medicine, while laying the foundations of all future vaccine development.

Not unsurprisingly, this method of treating patients by injection rapidly became very popular. It was a simple, safe, and effective way of providing protection against various harmful diseases, using the body's natural defences to build protection throughout life and at different ages, from birth to childhood, as teenagers and into old age.

It was not actually until a few years later that the term 'hypodermic' and 'hypodermic needle,' coined by London surgeon Charles Hunter, started to be used; the word hypodermic coming from the Greek words 'hypo' (under) and 'derma' (skin). The design of hypodermic needles and syringes today is little changed from that first developed by Wood.

Today, vaccines are said to prevent more than 20 life-threatening diseases, from diphtheria, tetanus, pertussis (whooping cough), influenza and measles, as well as their more recent success in Covid vaccinations.

EARLY EXPERIMENTS WITH ANAESTHETICS

It was in the early 1800s that surgeons started experimenting with chemicals to find an effective anaesthetic: Some of the first possible solutions included Laughing Gas (nitrous oxide), but this could not get rid of pain completely. Another possible chemical was Ether which had side effects that irritated the eyes and lungs, causing coughing and sickness.

A more effective anaesthetic was eventually found in 1847 by James Simpson, a professor of midwifery at the University of Edinburgh. Looking to find a better anaesthetic to ease the pain women experienced in childbirth, he was experimenting at home with his colleagues by inhaling different chemicals, eventually realising very quickly that chloroform was an effective anaesthetic. However, not everything went smoothly; there was some opposition to the use of chloroform; some surgeons preferred their patients to stay awake so that they could fight for their lives, while some religious leaders believed God intended for humans to experience pain, especially in childbirth.

By inventing an inhaler to measure the dosage given he was able to control the rate of chloroform inhalation. In 1854, Queen Victoria used chloroform during the birth of one of her children. This led to its usage being more widely accepted in Great Britain and throughout the counties.

The following year, In 1848, John Snow, a physician in London, went on to discover that cholera spread in sewage-tainted water. His findings soon led to changes in sanitation and water supply that finally brought to an end the cholera epidemics that had been occurring in England, Europe and Americas.

THE USE OF ANTISEPTICS TO REDUCE DEATH RATES IN OPERATIONS

While advances were taking place in pain killers, in vaccinations, in anaesthetics and surgery during the early and middle 1800s, not all the causes of illness and death during surgery had been eliminated. Surgeons sometimes still wore dirty clothes to the operating theatre.

Hand washing before operating was not always done. Why? Because it was not known that bacteria was the major cause of infection and death in operations.

Significant progress only came about when antiseptics were first discovered in 1867 by a surgeon called Joseph Lister. Lister knew about Pasteur's germ theory and went on to discover that carbolic acid killed the bacteria in open wounds. His discoveries led him to recommend that: doctors and nurses should wash their hands in carbolic acid before any operation; that bandages and ligatures should be soaked in carbolic acid; that a carbolic spray should be used to clean all the areas where an operation would be taking place.

Lister used all these methods in his surgical operations and the death rate in his operations fell from 46 per cent to 15 per cent. By the late 1800s, Lister's antiseptic methods of killing the germs on a wound had led to the introduction of aseptic surgery. This meant that even more germs were removed from the operating theatre, with the aim of creating a totally germ-free environment.

Lister's aseptic surgery included many different aspects, including the thorough cleaning of operating theatres before and after surgery; the frequent cleaning of other areas of a hospital; surgeons wearing sterilised gowns, masks and gloves; and all surgical instruments being sterilised before use using steam.

ANTIBACTERIAL CHEMICALS IN ACTION

It wasn't until towards the end of the 1800s that scientists first began to observe antibacterial chemicals in action. In Germany, Robert Koch developed the science of bacteriology and identifying the bacteria which caused anthrax and cholera, while physician Paul Ehrlich, a student of Koch, had concluded that it must be possible to create substances that could selectively kill bacteria without harming other cells.

This led him in the early 1900s to create the first modern antibiotic, producing the drug Salvarsan that became widely used to treat syphilis, followed a couple of decades later by Alexander Fleming, Professor of Bacteriology at St. Mary's Hospital in London, who accidentally discovered penicillin, the first true antibiotic. This was first isolated in 1942, subsequently revolutionizing the treatment of bacterial infections. But more about these developments in subsequent chapters.

ONE OF THE FIRST SYMBOLS OF A MORE MODERN APPROACH TO MEDICINE

Before concluding this chapter examining some of the key 19th century developments that have made a significant impact on life expectancy, medicines and medical treatments, it is perhaps worth mentioning a relatively simple medical device invented in 1816 that went on to become one of the most critical symbols of 19th, 20th and even current, healthcare professionals – the stethoscope. Invented by René Laennec, this one piece of medical equipment, is often regarded as having the highest positive impact on how the trustworthiness of doctors and other medical practitioners is perceived.

Laennec's stethoscope, developed because he wasn't comfortable placing his ear onto a woman's chest, consisted of, initially, a rolled

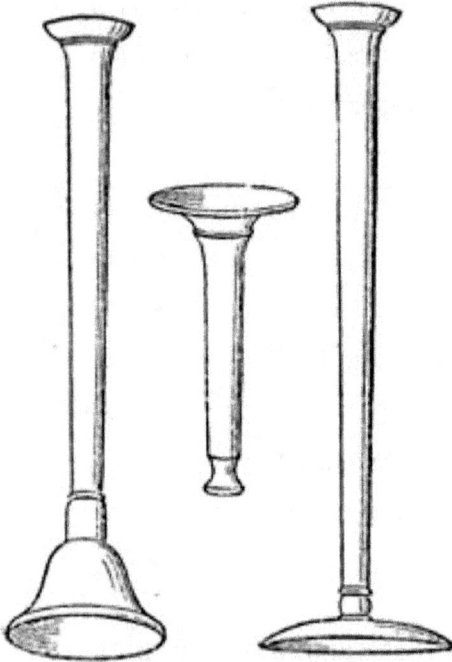

Hörrohr (Stethoskop).

Images of early stethoscopes.

paper tube, and then evolving into a wooden tube more suitably designed for listening to internal sounds from the heart and lungs in the human body. It was some 25 years later that the first stethoscope with an earpiece for each year was developed in New York. The modern stethoscopes of today come from the 1960s when Dr. David Littman patented a revolutionary new instrument with vastly improved acoustical performance.

Acquired and further refined and improved by 3M, Littman's stethoscopes are today used by millions of doctors and medical professionals worldwide.

EVER-MORE PATENT AND QUACK MEDICATIONS

While there were many key advances in treatment, cleanliness, pain relief and anaesthetics taking place in the early and middle years of the 1800s, there were still all kinds of new medications, pills and potions appearing in the Kent newspaper advertisements of the time, such as this extract from the *Kentish Gazette* in 1801 and headed DIXON'S ANTIBILIOUS PILLS.

In this advertisement it claimed that 'public testimony to the efficacy of Dixon's Pills had added to the successful and extensive private practice that the Proprietor of an apothecary had experienced in the high circle in their use, pointing them out as the 'most safe and convenient medicine for the removal of all Bilious complaints, and for those disorders which arise from irregular secretion of bile, often produced by free drinking; during pregnancy they are eminently serviceable in preventing costiveness, sickness at the stomach, nervous head-aches, heart burn, and those uneasinesses which too frequently attack the fair sex at that delicate period.'

The pills were packaged in boxes containing a statement of efficacy wrapped around each box signed by G Dixon, and sealed with his arms. They were sold in Kent by Simmons and Kirkby, and Bristow's, both in Canterbury, and by other respectable medicine vendors, in boxes at 5s. 5d., and 9s. 9d. each.

With more and more medicines, pills, ointments and creams available for purchase by households, between them claiming to be able to cure almost any known ailment, It was perhaps not surprising that yet another updated domestic medical book, following on from other similar medicine books from the late 1700s, mostly on the prevention and cure of diseases and the use of simple medicines, should be published. The latest version, written by an eminent Scottish physician, was illustrated with elegant copper plates, and promoted with an advertisement in The *Kentish Gazette* dated December 1801. This described the book as:

'An Entire New Domestic Medicine. BUCHAN-DOMESTIC MEDICINE. Considerably enlarged and improved, by an eminent Physician. Illustrated with elegant Copper Plates, and now to be published in Weekly Numbers, Price only Is. each.'

It went on to say: 'This day is published, NUMBER I. Embellished with an elegant Frontispiece, and another Copper Plate properly adapted to the subject (the whole to be completed in only Twelve Numbers, including all the improvements, additions, and alterations) of THE NEW Domestic Medicine: or, Universal Family Physician.' The book contained a complete Treatise on the Prevention and Cure of Diseases Regimen and Simple Medicines. with an Appendix, and containing a Dispensatory for the use of Private Practitioners.

'To which are now added, Observations on the Diet of the Common People; recommending a method of living less expensive, and more conducive to health, than the present.'

Move forward a few years to the 1808 period and the *Kentish Weekly Post* or *Canterbury Journal* on 8th April, 1808, carried the following advertisement:

Headed STRENGHENING PILLS. Prepared by Dr. HARMSTRONG. These pills were said to 'cure Asthmas and Shortness of Breathing, Abscesses on the Lungs, Female Weaknesses of every description, bearing down of the Womb from bad Labours,

Seminal Weakness in Men, Sprains by lifting, or other causes; and as a bracer of the Solids, and a Promoter of Digestion.' It also noted that the pills were kept as a Family Medicine by the first persons of distinction in the kingdom, and were strongly recommended by the most eminent physicians to sea bathers, and for debility in either sex. Price 6s. the box, duty included.

THE ONLY MEDICINE IN THE WORLD FOR CURING INFLAMMATIONS

Immediately following the above advertisement was a further entry aimed at the female market, namely for Dr. Harmstrong's FEMALE MENSTRUATED VEGETABLE PILLS, 'for females only at the commencement and decline of the most critical period of their lives, and is the most proper physic for Women after lying-in, or miscarriages, being the only Medicine in the World to be depended on for curing Inflammations, Obstructions and Ulcers in the Womb.'

Dr Harmstrong's Pills were available from his surgery in West Smithfield; and from retail outlets in Canterbury, Chatham, Rochester, Gravesend, Maidstone, Dover, Deal, Faversham, Ramsgate, Margate, Sandwich, Tunbridge Wells, Malling, Dartford, Sittingbourne and Hythe.

Dr. Harmstrong's Pills certainly looked to be aiming for much the same market as Dr. John Hooper's Famous Female Pills that had first appeared in the 1700s. But why such an interest during the 1700s and early 1800s in female complaints, miscarriages and childbirth? Quite simply, childbirth at this time was the greatest risk to a woman's health and the single most common cause of death right up until the introduction of anaesthetics and antibiotics. There was a near 30 percent mortality rate for the mother during childbirth, while something like 15 percent of babies – even if they survived the birth – died before their first birthday. Providing a new born girl did survive beyond the first year, she was not expected to live beyond her 43rd birthday, by which time the average woman would have already given birth to around six to eight children, assuming she survived each of the births.

A MEDICINE THAT CAN NEVER DO HARM

Outside of women's complaints and treatments, there were all kinds of other medicines still being introduced to the public in Kent newspapers, such as this one from the *Kentish Weekly Post* or *Canterbury Journal* from 10th December, 1802, headed 'WINTER MEDICINE CHEST. THE BALSAM of LIQUORICE, a small bottle of which contains all the pectoral properties of a whole pound of Liquorice Root, divested of its gross and superfluous parts; may be relied on as an agreeable and expeditious remedy for Complaints of the Lungs, as Coughs, Colds, Hoarseness, Wheezings, and even in the most obstinate Asthmas, Hooping Cough, or Pulmonary Consumptions, it will effect all that can rationally be expected from any Medicine; it has also this decided advantage over many preparations extolled for the cure of Coughs, (some of which contain large doses of Laudanum) that although it is unquestionably a most efficacious and pleasant pectoral, yet its composition is so simple and innocent that it can never do harm; the Proprietor being a regular bred Surgeon it is warranted in making this public declaration.'

If this medicine wasn't enough to cure winter coughs and colds, it was immediately followed in the same newspaper by a further cough and cold remedy, namely MANN'S APPROVED MEDICINE, for violent Coughs, Colds, Asthmas, Consumptions, Hooping Cough, Convulsions, and Debilitated Constitutions. Sold as The Great Restorative to Health, the medicine sold in bottles at 2s. 6d. and 4s. 6d. each, duty included, with the name of the inventor, in his own hand, on each bill of directions.

A further advertisement in the newspaper was used to inform the Public that Mr. W. Bristow, Canterbury, had received a fresh supply of THE NERVINE CORDIAL PILLS, which were 'particularly recommended to those who have injured their constitutions by inordinate passions, and excesses in irregular indulgences, or other debilitative causes, creative of a weakened or relaxed state of the solids, loss of strength, lowness of spirits, horrors of the mind, trembling of the limbs, &c. as one Box is sufficient to prove their invigorating and cordial properties, when taken at night.'

All of these three medicines were available from their respective proprietors in London, from Bristow's in Canterbury, or sold wholesale and retail throughout Kent, with the advertisement noting that none of the vender's sales of these medicines should be regarded as genuine, unless they had been signed with red ink by the Proprietor.

Another *Kentish Gazette* advertisement from 17 November 1809 was for ANTISPASMODIC PILLS, which offered a certain cure for Epilepsy, or Falling Sickness, Convulsion Fits, Hysteric and Paralytic Affections, and offering an infallible antidote of that MORTAL MALADY, THE APOPLEXY.

A VOGUE FOR COLOURED PILLS

Looking at Kent newspapers from the 1820s sees yet more pills and potions being advertised in almost every issue, such as this one from the *Kentish Weekly Post* or *Canterbury Journal* of 29th September, 1829, for DR. BOERHAAVE'S RED PILL, considered 'a specific cure for every stage and symptom of VENERAL DISEASE as it eradicates them without confinement or inconvenience, and is found equally safe, speedy and efficient.' It went on to say that many thousands had been enabled by it to cure themselves with secrecy and despatch, and its increasing sale, bears testimony to its great efficacy. Boxes of pills (price 4. 6d. and sealed with red wax) sold by R. Colgate, Canterbury, and all medicine vendors.

Coloured pills seem to be very much the rage of the 1820s, with the *Southern Gazette* of April 1827 carrying an advertisement for DR.

CULLENS celebrated SCARLET PILL. These were claimed to be the Most Infallible Preventative Cure of Certain Disease Ever Discovered. These pills were strongly recommended to those who went on long journeys, and to 'seafaring gentlemen, who cannot supply themselves with a more safe, useful or convenient remedy for the eradication of the deadly disease, Distemper, without the aid of medical assistance.'

Dr. Cullen's Pills were sold by all booksellers and respectable Patent Medicine Vendors in the United Kingdom, at 2s. 9d. a sealed box and containing full and plain instructions. Purchasers were noted to observe that the boxes of pills were not genuine unless they contained the SCARLETT PILLS stamp (as shown at the bottom of the advertisement).

The same newspaper edition also printed an advert for MANN'S APPROVED MEDICINE, Recommended by Physicians, and patronised by Ladies and Gentlemen of the first distinction; sold in bottles at 2s. 6d., duty included, and engraved on the stamp with 'THOMAS MANN Horsham, Sussex, the Inventor and sole Proprietor.' The medicine was claimed to restore when all hopes of recovery have been given up in consumption, coughs, colds, influenza, dropsy, relaxed habits, hooping cough, and in low nervous debilitated states.

AN ABSOLUTELY SAFE AND CERTAIN CURE FOR THE ITCH

Another interesting product that was claimed in Kent newspaper advertising in the early 1800s 'to be so effectual that, when applied according to the instructions, it had never been known to fail of curing even the worst cases.' Headed FOR THE ITCH, DR. FREEMAN'S OINTMENT, it claimed to be the only absolutely safe and certain cure, by one single application, for that disagreeable disorder The Itch, to which, from its infectious nature, all classes of society are daily liable.

The advertisement went on to state that 'In order to place this ointment within reach of the poorer classes, it is sold at the low price of one shilling and three halfpence the box, which is sufficient for dressing one grown person, or two young children, and may be procured from the newspaper printer, I. Pickering, Margate, and from Principal Druggists and Medicine Vendors in every Kent town.'

If it wasn't problems with itching that needed curing, then what about immediate relief from nervous complaints and debility by using FOTHEGILL'S NERVOUS DROPS. Advertised in the *Kentish Weekly Post* or *Canterbury Journal* on the 30th June 1829, the drops were promoted 'To those who are afflicted with Nervous disorders and their distressing affect ions as oppression of Spirits, Head Aches, loss of Appetite, Indigestion, Spasms, Tremors, Fainting Fits, and Debility or Relaxation of the System, is confidently recommended to have recourse to the above celebrated Medicine from which they are assured to obtaining immediate relief, and by perseverance in It agreeably to the directions given, the complete re-establishment of their health.'

Sold in bottles at 4s. 6d.; 11s; and 22s. by the principal Medicine Vendors, of whom may also be had FOTHERGILL's TONIC FEMALE PILLS, recommended in general Debility of the Constitution as a safe and excellent remedy in those periodical irregularities which Females, of delicate and languid circulation, more especially the younger part, are liable to. Sold in boxes at 1s. 1½d., and 2s. 9d.

Rather different to the usual advertisements for pills, medicines and all kinds of potions were the occasional advertisements for medical products, such as a particular advertisement that regularly appeared in the 1820s in Kent newspapers and aimed at patients with difficult cases of rupture. This was headed as follows:

PINDIN'S PATENT TRUSSES.

WITHOUT METALLIC SPRINGS.

SURGEONS of the first eminence in Town and Country having experienced in their own Patients that even the most difficult cases of Rupture can be kept up, by the above TRUSSES. Available from GAWAN & CO. of 200, Fleet-street, (just doors from Temple Bar), London, or selected Kent retailers.

Weaknesses of the stomach were also featured in an advertisement in the *Kentish Weekly Post* or *Canterbury Journal* of 5th April 1822. This featured an Approved Remedy for Weakness of the Stomach, Persons of Bilious Habits, or those who are subject to Indigestion, Loss of Appetite, Sickness, Pains, and Complaints in the Stomach and Bowels, or other symptoms resulting from a weakened or deranged state of the digestive organs.

Readers of the advertisement were earnestly recommended to make use of TOWERS'S TONIC PILLS, as one of lie safest and most certain remedies ever recommended to the public notice. 'Mild, but effective in their operation, they cleanse, and yet strengthen the stomach, restore the appetite, promote digestion, and keep the bowels in a regular and comfortable state, free from costiveness but no means too relaxed.' The Tonic Pills could be procured (at 3s. 9d., 4s. 6d., 10s., and 22s., per box,) of H. Christian, Canterbury, and all other Vendors of genuine Medicines, wholesale and retail, throughout the United Kingdoms.

THE USE OF ASTONISHING TESTIMONIALS

Study the many advertisements so far mentioned in this book and it's particularly noticeable that so many of them make quite astonishing claims about their respective pills or medicines. Claims such as 'Offers a certain cure,' or 'The only medicine in the world to be depended on for curing inflammation,' and yet others that say 'Restores when all hope of recovery have been given up,' or 'Never been known to fail.'

A label on a Fever Cure and Stomachic Mixture medicine bottle (illustrated) from the late 1800s states that it is 'A well-known and Highly Approved Remedy for Fevers, Sore Throats, Influenza, Bad Colds, and especially useful in Sickness, Disordered Stomach and Bowel Complaints,' while also noting 'The preparation is recommended for its efficiency by hundreds of users.' The price was 1s. per bottle.

Such claims as quoted in the paragraphs above, were still being widely made in advertisements and packaging in the late 1840s, but now also started to carry one, two, three or more testimonials from satisfied customers in every box, and sometimes in advertising as well, while also cautioning purchasers, such as in this advertisement for EYRE'S Cough Pills from the *South Eastern Gazette* in September

1848. This stated: 'Notice to the PUBLIC' — Numerous mistakes having occurred with some vendors of EYRE'S COUGH PILLS, the proprietors deem it prudent to caution purchasers of this Medicine to particularly notice the words on the label "AS PREPARED BY MR. D. EYRE, Surgeon, Lee, Kent." They are wrapped in buff paper.'

Mr Eyre was obviously unhappy with some competitor advertising as his own advertisement urged readers to 'Ask for: SURGEON EYRE'S PECTORAL PILLS.' stating that the pills required only one Dose to be taken to prove their efficacy, and adding that a Box would relieve a person troubled with the most obstinate Cough, of whatever duration, and in most instances effect a permanent cure.

Further on in the advertisement, under yet another heading for EYRE'S COUGH PILLS, his message continued by stating 'It is not by advertising these Pills that

SPECIAL

FEVER CURE

AND

STOMACHIC MIXTURE

P. J. F. 164 (20).

A well-known and Highly approved Remedy for Fevers, Sore Throats, Influenza, Bad Colds, and especially useful in Sickness, Disordered Stomach and Bowel Complaints, &c., &c.

This preparation is recommended for its efficiency by hundreds of users.

1/- per Bottle.

PREPARED BY

G. HEUGHAN, M.P.S.

Dispensing Chemist.

8, KINGSWAY (off Northgate)

DEWSBURY.

Tel. 593.

Mr. Eyre, Surgeon, Lee, Kent, has deservedly received so many astonishing Testimonials, which are enclosed with every Box, but by the recommendation of Mr. E.'s Patients, who have been cured of the following complaints, viz., Incipient Consumption, Asthma, Coughs, Shortness of Breath, &c.' Then it continued by claiming that it was a well known fact, that numbers of our fellow creatures are sacrificed through taking compounds prepared by uneducated men in the practice of Physic. The sufferer commences from having seen it advertised in numerous publications and without finding the least relief whatever, is induced to continue it, being in hope that he will shortly benefit, which unfortunately ends in a fruitless attempt.

The advertisement finally ended with the message that MANY EXCELLENT MEDICINES have been discovered by medical men for various complaints; but because Pills are introduced by advertisers, some of whom are totally unacquainted with the profession, a gentleman who has been educated for it considers it disgraceful, consequently comparatively few have the benefit of a good discovery of this kind. The advertisement ended with 'It 'is this and the Testimonials, that have induced Mr. Eyre to present the recipe of the Pills to the present Proprietor; and with the strongest confidence he recommends them, after using the same in his practice for more than forty-seven years.'

TREATMENT FOR THE PREMATURE DECLINE OF MANHOOD

Much has been made in this and other chapters about the various treatments available for female complaints, so it was quite interesting to find that immediately following the above advertisement for

Eyre's Cough Pills was an advertisement for a Medical Essay on MANHOOD: the CAUSES of its PREMATURE DECLINE, with plain DIRECTIONS for its PEFECT RESTORATION.

This went on to say the Medical Essay discussed the diseases of the generative organs, emanating from solitary and sedentary habits, indiscriminate excesses, the effects of climate and infection, &c., and was addressed to the sufferer in youth, manhood, and old age; with practical remarks on marriage, the treatment and cure of nervous and mental debility, impotence, syphilis, and other urino-genital diseases, by which even the most shattered constitutions may be restored, and reach the full period of life allotted.

A number of reviews of the book followed, notably one said to be from the *Chronicle* that wrote: 'To the gay and thoughtless we trust this little work will serves as a beacon, to warn them of the danger attendant upon the too rash indulgence of their passions, whilst to some it may serve as a monitor in the hour of temptation, and to the afflicted as a sure guide of health.'

The book was on-sale priced 3s. 0d. in Maidstone by Mr. J. Smith, Bookseller and Publisher, 10 Week Street; by Colegate, Canterbury; Dunkin and Son, Dartford; Houghton, Dover; Hopkins, New Road, Gravesend; or sent enclosed in a sealed envelope, post paid, for 3s. 6d.

Immediately following this book announcement were brief details of the TWENTY-FIFTH EDITION of a book entitled PHYSICAL DISQUALIFICATIONS, GENERATIVE INCAPACITY, AND IMPEDIMENTS TO MARRIAGE, which was illustrated by 20 Anatomical Coloured Engravings in 196 pages. Just published, price 2s. 6d., or by post direct at 3s. 6d., in postage stamps.

A further book on the same newspaper page was entitled CONTROL OF THE PASSIONS, described as a practical treatise addressed to youth on the indiscretions that produce unfeeble conditions of health and diminish duration of human life, and containing instructions for the perfect restoration from the evil consequences of syphilitic infection. The book was priced at 1s. 6d..

MULTIPLE ADVERTISEMENTS FOR SKIN AND TEETH REMEDIES

While earlier newspapers from the 1700s and early 1800s usually only carried one or two promotions for pills, medicines and treatments, its noticeable that by the middle 1800s there could be multiple advertisements for all kinds of remedies, often mixed in with advertisements for everything from carpets to tea, coffee, soda water and lemonade, or brandy.

Taking the *South Easter Gazette* of 26th September 1848, it is possible to find advertising for ROWLANDS' KALYDOR, an Oriental Balsamic Preparation for purifying the skin from all pimples, spots, freckles, tan and discolorations, so producing a healthy freshness of complexion. as well as for ROWLANDS' ODONTO, a pearl white dentifrice for preserving teeth and gums, and to give sweetness to the breath. It claimed to have been selected by the Queen, the Court, and Royal Family of Great Britain, and several Sovereigns and Courts of Europe.

Another tooth treatment being promoted on the same page was for BRANDE'S IMPERIAL ENAMEL for stopping decaying teeth, preventing tooth-ache, and improving mastication. The method of treatment was described as 'put the enamel into the tooth in a soft state, which then becomes hard in a few minutes. Applied with ease without any pain.'

A further tooth treatment, headed CAUTION TO MOTHERS, was for MRS. JOHNSON'S AMERICAN SOOTHING SYRUP for children CUTTING THEIR TEETH. This claimed to be an infallible remedy that had preserved hundreds of children, when thought past recovery from convulsions arising from painful dentition, noting that as soon as the syrup was applied on the gums, the child would be relived, the gums cooled, and the inflammation reduced.

It is perhaps worth noting that dentistry in the 1800s was still very much in its infancy, with a demand for false teeth already starting to grow. By the later 1700s and early 1800s there were all kinds of trades dabbling in dentistry: jewellers, blacksmiths, wigmakers, chemists, surgeons and ivory turners, with some of the early 'dentists' placing human teeth (sometimes extracted from the dead, or sold by the poor) into dentures.

When human teeth were scare, ivory and porcelain were used, both of which tended to yellow with age, so weren't as popular. The answer was to enamel them, as noted in the Arrowsmith, Surgeon Dentist advertisement shown here. For the more wealthy clients, gold springs would be installed so that the false teeth pressed against the gums and could be opened for speaking. However, most of these early forms of dentures were not designed for eating, at which time they would be removed.

MEDICAL AND OTHER TREATMENTS ALONGSIDE HOUSEHOLD PRODUCTS

Mixed in with the advertised medical products above, and others for cures for Hooping Cough, or Bilious and Liver complaints, can be found other advertisements for Carpets, Furniture and Upholstery; for Black tea, Congou tea, Souchong tea and Lapsan tea; Ceylon coffee, Java coffee, Mocha coffee; Brandy; Soda water, Lemonade and other aerated waters , these last products noted as by special appointment to Her Majesty and all the Royal Family.

Perhaps one of the more intriguing of the advertisements mixed in with all the other products on the Kent newspaper pages, was a summary of a book treatise on LOVE, described as 'the leading feeling of the human breast; more exalted than mere passion, stronger than avarice, more engrossing than ambition, for which no man is exempt from its influence, or can avoid its sway.' The treatise was said to be the result of a long course of study in a peculiar and much neglected branch of medical practice, the author having obtained the highest medical honours, namely Doctor of Medicine, matriculated member of the University of Edinburgh, licentiate of Apothecaries Hall, honorary member of the London Hospital Medical Society.

The book was available for a price of 2s. 6d. from Mr. Smith, 10 Week Street, Maidstone; Mr Williams, Cannon Street, Dover.

So far, study has only been made of the many different medicines, pills and treatments up to the mid 1800s, their uses, recommendations and testimonials, but did this pattern of medical advances continue in the later years of the 1800s?

NEW MEDICINES AND TREATMENTS AND GROWING INTEREST IN HOMEOPATHY

The later decades of the 1800s, from the 1850s onwards, sees a continued and growing interest in all kinds of new curative medicines, in homeopathic and vegetable treatments, in new medical and dental products, in custom-designed artificial limbs, as well as a rise in specialist treatment advertising (feet, teeth, hair, stomach, urinary tract, female) by surgeons, doctors, chemists, dentists, chiropodists, etc., and the founding, growth and marketing of pills by the new drug companies that had been formed, such as Beecham's.

Such was the growth in the advertising of medicines, products and treatments that Kent newspapers by 1850 are carrying multiple entries for all kinds of medicinal, dental and hair products and services, many often apparently competing against rival advertisers for the treatment of coughs and colds, stomach and liver complaints, false teeth or, increasingly, sexual diseases. They are also trying to outdo each other in terms of the claims that they make or in the testimonials provided.

Perhaps a good example of such advertising is to examine just one page in the *South Eastern Gazette* of the 7th May, 1850. What do we find being promoted? Everything from Brodie's Purifying Vegetable Pills; Matthews's Opiated Chloroform Liniment; Holloway's Pills for the liver and stomach; The Cordial Balm of Syriacum; Spencer's Pulmonic Elixer; Parr's Life Pills; Wordsdell's Vegetable Restorative Pills; The Revalenta Arabica Food; and Woolley's Pectoral Candy – and that's not all of the announcements. So what are some of the conclusions that can be drawn from these entries?

RISING INTEREST IN HOMEOPATHIC, HERB, PLANT AND VEGETABLE TREATMENTS

The use of plant-based medicines had been a staple of the county's alchemists and dispensaries for many centuries, although not always described as such in their various descriptions. The main difference in the 1850s onwards is that being plant-based was now seen as a key selling and marketing attraction for purchasers, with a dedicated Homeopathic Dispensary already open from the mid-1800s for the admission of patients in both Snargate Street, Dover, and High Street, Folkestone.

Just a few years later the *Dover Telegraph* and *Cinque Ports Advertiser* in June 1857, carried an advertisement for 'HOMEOPATHIC MEDICINES. PATENT MEDICINES. Farina's Eau de Cologne, Eau de Botot. Tooth brushes, 4d., 6d., 8d., and 1s. each. Domestic tooth powder, 6d. per box.' It concluded with 'The Beckwith Sachet powder, highly approved for perfuming Boxes, writing desks, paper, &e., 1s. per ounce. BATHING CAPS. BOLTON, 10, KING STREET, DOVER.'

Kent newspapers at this time were already carrying various announcements for vegetable and herb-based medications. R. J. BRODIE'S PURIFYING VEGETABLE PILLS for example, as advertised in the *South Eastern Gazette* in 1850, were promoted as being prepared from 'the most choice of vegetable productions, and differed materially from all other preparations, as they are warranted not to contain a particle of mercury, Cubebs (a native plant of Indonesia used for parasitic infections), or any other deleterious drug.'

The same newspaper also carried an advertisement with the heading 'TRIUMPHS OF MEDICINE,' followed by 'This MEDICINE wroughts the most wonderful cures, and has conferred upon Families an incalculable amount of benefit for the justly celebrated WORSDELL'S VEGETABLE RESTORATIVE PILLS, prepared solely by John Kaye, Esq., of Dalton Hall, near Huddersfield.'

The advertisement continued with 'The overwhelming mass of facts which has gone forth from time to time demonstrate that, for purifying the blood, removing obstructions, causing the fluids to flow in their natural order; aiding digestion, relieving the head from oppressiveness, and imparting health and vigour to the whole system, so that it may perform all its functions with tone and energy, no remedy so effectual for the removal of pain and disease was ever presented to the notice of the public. No person can take them without deriving benefit, and that in a short space of time, unlike other medicines, they are harmless in their nature, while powerful in their operation.'

A further advertisement in the same newspaper was headed 'NO MORE PILLS OR ANY OTHER MEDICINE,' and was promoting The Revalenta Arabica Food, which 'without medicine of any kind, speedily and permanently removes dyspepsia, constipation and diarrhoea, nervousness, biliousness, affections of the liver and kidneys, flatulency, distension, palpitations of the heart, deafness, noises in the head and ears, consumption, dropsy, rheumatism, gout, heartburn, nausea and vomiting during pregnancy, spasms, paralysis, coughs, asthma, sleeplessness, involuntary blushing, tremors, dislike to society, loss of memory, delusions, vertigo, exhaustion, thoughts of self destruction and insanity.' It also claimed to be the only food that never turns acid on the weakest stomach, but imparts a healthy relish and restores the faculty of digestion.' It appears as if the medicine can cure pretty-well any known ailment.

In reality, Revalenta Arabica was a widely used name given to a preparation of the common lentil (its first name being formed by the transposition of letters its earlier botanical name, "Ervum lens") and which was often sold as an empirical diet for invalids but, as seen above, with extraordinary restorative virtues being attributed to it. The newspaper advertisement also include a long list of quite extravagant testimonials, as well as the name and town of suppliers throughout Kent.

A further advertisement on the same newspaper page was for THE CORDIAL BALM OF SYRIACUM, a widely used herbal medicinal plant found and used in the Middle East over many centuries and which had been found to be beneficial in the treatment of various diseases such as cancer, peptic ulcers and neurodegenerative disorders. It had many medicinal properties, such as antimicrobial, antioxidant, anti-inflammatory, anti-fungal, antispasmodic and anti-cancer.

BRANDY RECOMMENDED BY BOARD OF HEALTH FOR MEDICAL TREATMENT

Further study of the *South Eastern Gazette* in May 1850 finds an interesting announcement TO THE GUARDIANS OF THE UNION, and others having CHARGE OF THE POOR which is found recommending the use of BRANDY as a Medical Treatment.

This announcement stated that 'THE BOARD OF HEALTH having in their first circular recommended the use of Brandy in the Medical Treatment of persons labouring under the premonitory symptoms of Cholera, we think it right to publish the following important Testimonials in favour of our Patent Brandy, which has long been employed in preference to Foreign for medicinal purposes, at St. George's St. Thomas's, Guy's, and the Westminster Hospitals, and also in the Manchester, Bristol, and Brighton Infirmaries.'

Underneath this announcement was the heading EXTRACTS FROM TESTIMONIALS, followed by, firstly, "Your Patent Brandy contains as pure a spirit fund in the best varieties Foreign Brandy. (Signed) Edward Turner, Professor of Chemistry, London University." Then, "Your Patent Brandy Is free from uncombined acids, which exist, more or less, in most of the Brandies imported from France. (Signed) John Thomas Cooper, Professor, Guy's Hospital and Grenadier Guards Hospital," and finally by "The two samples of your Patent Brandy I had an opportunity of laying before the Board of Officers, which sat at the Regimental Hospital last Saturday. Every member of the Board approved of the Brandy, and I have ordered that it shall be used at the Hospital for the sick. (Signed) J. Harrison, Surgeon-Major, Grenadier Guards."

The advertisement was signed off as BETTS & CO., PATENT BRANDY DISTILLERS, London, and noting that The Patent Brandy, in combination with Ginger, may be had on the same terms, if preferred.

MAJOR 19TH CENTURY MILESTONE IN THE HISTORY OF PHARMACY AND DRUG USE

Already set out in previous pages, the various advances in drug discoveries in the middle and late 1800s meant that more potent – and more dangerous – medicines had been finding their way into people's homes, with pressure growing for some kind of Regulation to be introduced. The first national piece of legislation to regulate the sale of medicines had been introduced with the 1851 Arsenic Act. This initial Act required that a register had to be kept of all sales, that the buyer had to be known to the seller and that arsenic had to be coloured with a substance such as soot or indigo.

Arsenic, of course, was not the only dangerous substance being used medicinally and it was therefore decided that legislation needed to go even further. It was then that the Pharmaceutical Society proposed new regulations that would ensure the safer use of medicines and better protect the public. The result was that in July 1868 the Pharmacy Act was passed in Great Britain, which gave the Society the power to decide which potentially dangerous medicinal substances would be classified as poisons, and 15 poisons were named in the original legislation.

It also gave instructions detailing how poisons should be labelled and limited their sale to persons registered with the Society, with the qualification being that they should have passed one of the School of Pharmacy's examinations. The Society's system of pharmacy education was then rolled out to everyone that had a responsibility for selling dangerous medicines to the public, including morphine and any preparation of opium which, as has been previously

90

mentioned in earlier chapters, were popular products in the druggists' stores and in home medicinal cupboards.

AVAILABILITY OF MEDICAL APPLIANCES AND ARTIFICIAL LIMBS

From the late fifteenth right through to the nineteenth centuries, a variety of custom-designed limbs were built following the loss of legs, arms, hand, fingers, toes. These could results from farm, coaching or manufacturing accidents, from animals, or from wars, falls, etc. The resulting artificial limbs were made of combinations of wood, metal, leather, and other materials, some of the designs being fantastic examples of craftsmanship. Many were controlled by cables, gears, cranks, and springs, and could often be rotated and

A 1930s advertisement by a maker of surgical appliances.
Illustration courtesy of SJAAdvertArchive/Alamy Stock Photo

bent. There were even prosthetic fingers made to grip objects.

By the late 19th century, various prosthetics vendors would offer quite basic peglegs as cheaper alternatives to the more intricate and quite lifelike artificial arms and legs that had now become available. While limb manufacturers touted the advantages of more complicated prostheses over the simpler peglegs, it was said that, according to a contemporary surgeon, many patients actually found a pegleg more comfortable for walking – but all limbs needed proper fitting, as noted in this advertisement from the *Faversham Times and Mercury*, 17th August 1867.

The advertisement was headed 'ARTIFICIAL LIMBS.' This then goes on to note that 'Those, who unfortunately require artificial limbs are requested to notice that the MAKER, and not the VENDOR, is the proper person to ensure a fit and durable article. The Artificial Leg for above the knee £8. 8s. to £10; for below from £5 to £10; Pin Leg with joint £2. 5s. to £3. Artificial Hand (India rubber) and Arm, £2. 10s. to £6. For circular of references send to Mr. Welton, 13, Grafton Street, Fitzroy Square, London.'

Apart from artificial limbs, there were also medical treatments for weak legs or arms and for those with varicose veins, such as seen in this advertisement in the *Dover Telegraph* in September 1856, for ELASTIC APPLIANCES FOR WEAK LEGS, KNEES, ANKLES, 6v., FOR VARICOSE VEINS. 'The material of which these articles are made, being very elastic and uniform in its pressure, is an excellent invention for giving efficient and permanent support in most cases of weakness, accompanied with swellings; also for varicose veins, sprains, and consequent weakness of the knees, wrists, ankles, &. They are light, durable, and may be easily cleaned without any lessening in their elasticity. The price of Stockings is 5s. 6d., 7s. 6d., and 10s. each, according to substance and quality. Knee-caps and Foot-pieces vary from 4s. to 7s. each.'

In 1891, a similar advertisement is placed in the *Kent Times* in May 1891, by George May of 82 Bank Street, Maidstone, and is again for a range of leg appliances, artificial limbs, knee caps, leg instruments for the correction of Club Foot, and for the Universal Truss, which can all be seen in this advertisement from the paper. At the end of the advert are notes that they are Appointed to the West Kent General Hospital, and that Mrs. May, who had had 21 years' experience, is available to attend to the Ladies Department, and at private residences if required.

Rather later in the 1800s, the *Gravesend & Northfleet Standard* in January 1897, is promoting 'TRUSSES, ELASTIC

STOCKINGS, ARTIFICIAL LIMBS, SURGICAL APPLIANCES, AT REDUCED PRICES. Go to the Actual Manufacturers, PACKHAM & Co., 20, KING ST., MAIDSTONE. Sole Manufacturers of Packham's Improved Slide Spring Self-Adjusting Truss. Prices from 3s. each. Perfect fit guaranteed. Makers of all kinds of trusses. Ladies and Gentlemen's Belts of all description made on the premises.

Another advertisement from the late 1800s was placed by J. BOLTON, Chemist and Druggist, 10 King Street, Dover, under the heading 'HOMOEOPATHETIC MEDICINES.' Concluding the announcement were the following additional medical products: 'ELASTIC SUPPORTING BELTS, of new construction, for Ladies to use before and after accouchement.' Finally, there was mention of 'INVALID WATER BEDS, CUSHIONS AND PILLOWS, for placing on ordinary bedsteads, supplied to order. They can be filled with hot or cold water, or inflated with air, and are found of great comfort to patients compelled to recline for long periods.'

The *Maidstone Journal* and *Kentish Advertiser* of 2nd June 1898, carries the following. 'The SURGICAL AID SOCIETY supplies Trusses, Elastic Stockings, Crutches, Artificial Eyes, Artificial Limbs, and every other description of mechanical support. Also Water beds and invalid chairs.'

Appointed by the above Surgical Aid Society for the fitting of Artificial Eyes was H. J. Drake, Practical and Consulting Optician, who advertised his services in the *Kent Times* in August 1897. His address was noted as 'Under the Clock, 12 Calverley Road, Tunbridge Wells.

94

ARTIFICIAL TEETH AND VARIOUS TOOTH AND HAIR PREPARATIONS

In other newspapers from the later years of the 1800s we find an advertisement by Mr. Quntin Hair, a Surgeon Dentist, with surgeries in Dover, Folkestone, Sandgate and Hythe, that is promoting his 'artificial teeth made by the aid of machinery,' as well as announcing a great reduction in prices of artificial teeth, and promoting his new and important discoveries.

A further small announcement in the paper was for Howard's Enamel for Decayed Teeth, however large the cavity, rendering extraction unnecessary, while the *Kent Times and Chronicle* in May 1891, carried an advertisement (shown on page 100) for PAINLESS DENTISTRY, using English and American Artificial Teeth, fitted painlessly without plates or wires by a combination of two of the latest inventions by Mr. J. Shipley Slipper, Surgeon Dentist. These inventions enabled artificial teeth to be fitted painlessly without extracting loose teeth or stumps. The teeth are said to be life-like in appearance, and can be adjusted without any injuries or wires, from 3s. 6d. per tooth. Attendance was made at Mr. J. Williams, Chemist

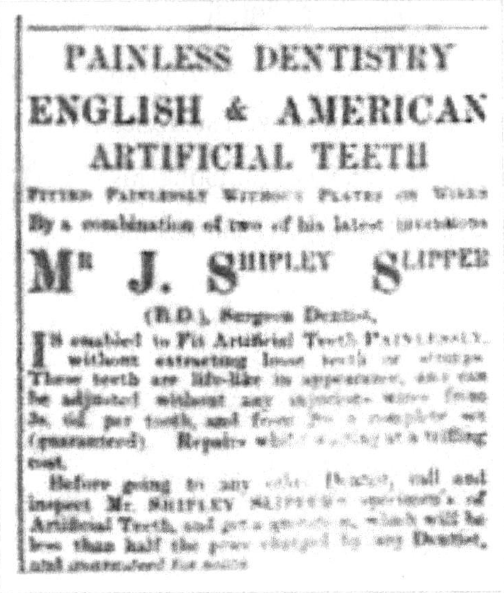
PAINLESS DENTISTRY
ENGLISH & AMERICAN
ARTIFICIAL TEETH
MR J. SHIPLEY SLIPPER
(R.D.), Surgeon Dentist,

in Tunbridge Wells every alternate Thursday.

Perhaps one of the more stranger advertisements appears in the late 1800s appears in the *Canterbury Journal*, *Kentish Times* and *Farmers' Gazette* in November 1899 which is headed: OLD FALSE TEETH BOUGHT and then goes on to announce 'Many ladies and gentlemen have by them old or disused false teeth, which might as well be turned into money. Messrs. R. D. & J. Fraser, of Princess Street, Ipswich, buy old false teeth. Send your teeth to them and they will remit you by return of post the utmost value or, if preferred, they will make you the best offer and hold the teeth over for your reply.'

While teeth-related advertisements feature quite commonly, so do announcements about various kinds of hair treatments, such as this one from the *Folkestone Express, Sandgate, Shorncliffe & Hythe Advertiser* of 3rd May 1879. Headed VALUABLE DISCOVERY FOR THE HAIR, it stated that 'If your hair is turning grey or white, or falling off, use "The Mexican Hair Restorer," for it will positively restore in every case grey or white hair to its original colour, without leaving the disagreeable smell of most Restorers. It makes the hair charmingly beautiful, as well as promoting the growth of hair on bald spots.'

In another advertisement from 1898, this time headed HAIR PREPARATIONS, it offered Medicate Oil; Preservative Balm (For rapidly producing new growth, and arresting the fall of the hair); Enutrient Cream, to prevent greyness; and various bottles of scurf and other creams. These were all available from Mr. Elkington, 1 King Street, Dover.

POPULAR MEDICINES FOR PURIFYING THE BLOOD

Towards the end of the 1800s there started to appear advertisements in various Kent newspapers for Clarke's Blood Mixture, which became a very popular medicine that was promoted in the media as a medical cure-all for a whole variety of 19th century ailments, such as sores, glandular swelling, skin complaints, scrofula, scurvy, cancerous ulcers, bad legs, rheumatism, gout, sore eyes, dropsy, pimples, blackheads and piles, noting 'its effects are marvellous.'

A three-time Mayor of Lincoln and noted philanthropist, Francis Jonathan Clarke (born in

1842) was concerned for the wellbeing of the people and this extended to a medicinal 'cure-all' in the form of his World Famed Blood Mixture, a remedy which promised great health benefits – but would not be able to pass muster in the 21st century. Even so, it was advertised as 'The Finest Blood Purifier that Science and Medical Skill have brought to light.'

Interestingly, when later analysed by the British Medical Association in 1909, the Blood Mixture was mainly found to contain a little water, a little sugar, a miniscule amount of alcohol, and traces of chloroform and ammonia – a medication whose medical benefits have been deemed to be somewhat questionable.

Another medication that appeared in Kent newspapers from the later years of the 1800s was for CONGREVE'S BALSAMIC ELIXIR, a New Treatment of Consumption and a popular medicinal remedy for everyone that suffered from chest diseases, including coughs, asthma, chronic bronchitis, and whooping cough. It was claimed to have accounts of nearly 400 successfully cured cases. The Elixir was sold in clear glass bottles with the name of the product embossed on them. An advertisement from The *Canterbury Journal* of September 4th 1899 for Congreve's Balsamic Elixir, is shown here courtesy of the British Newspaper Archive.

To this, can be added a preventative treatment for a variety of afflictions of the chest and throat, including colds, nasal catarrh, influenza and hay fever that can be seen in this label from a bottle of PYNOZONE, a germicidal inhalant sprinkled on to handkerchiefs and inhaled through the nostrils. Just 1s. a bottle. Prepared in Dewsbury and sold through chemists in towns throughout Kent.

So brings medications and treatments for the human population in the 1800s towards an end. Not every medication or advertisement has been looked at or reviewed.

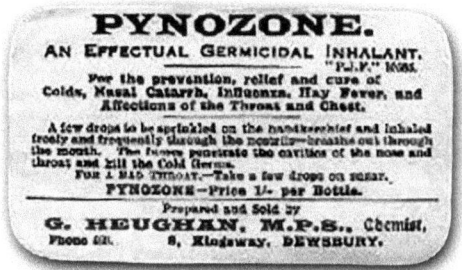

There were certainly many others that could possibly have been included, and a selection of many other medications found in chemists is shown in the large illustration found on page 100. It was a particularly interesting and important century for medical advances and a period which significantly started to extend life expectancy in childbirth and child life expectancy, reduced infections, made operations much safer, enabled vaccinations that moved to the elimination of certain viruses, and saw more effective artificial limbs, teeth and medical appliances.

However, before moving on, it is perhaps worth a final mention of an advertisement for some of the latest medications available for the veterinary specialist of the time, such as indicated in an

advertisement from the *Kent Times and Chronicle* in May 1891, for CUPISS CONSTITUTION BALLS for horse, cattle and sheep treatments that include those for grease, swelled legs, cracked heels, coughs, colds, etc., in horses; loss of appetite, distemper or influenza in cattle; and for scouring in calves.

The next chapter takes the reader into the early years of the 20th century.

MEDICINES AND NEW MEDICAL TREATMENTS IN THE EARLY 1900s

After researching newspaper archives covering more than 200 years, and studying medicines and treatments used in Kent to cure, or claim to cure, almost any ailment or illness, its time to bring this look at the history and evolution of treatments, medicines, pills and potions in Kent into the early years of the 20th century.

This was a period when there were all kinds of discoveries and medical advances, many from science-based developments, that were now changing the face of medicine and medical treatments almost beyond recognition and taking the life expectancy of women – a primary indicator of health education, housing and nutrition – from around 43 years way back in the late 1700s, and still only around 52 in 1900, right up to some 77 years of age by the 1980s.

Having said that, many of the medicines already mentioned in earlier chapters and dating from the 1800s, were still being promoted in 20th century Kent newspapers, often with much larger advertisements, and many of them listing an every-increasing number of chemists shops throughout Kent where the medications could be purchased. Indeed, a number of chemists now started advertising in their

Sell Your Cold for 1

DR. MACKENZIE'S

CATARRH-CURE

SMELLING BOTTLE

will cure it. It instantly Relieves and Cures Colds in the Head; Arrests Influenza; Removes Nervous Headaches relieves Hay Fever and Neuralgia in the Head. Is the best remedy for Faintness and Dizziness.

Sold by all Chemists and Stores, Price 1s.; or if you cannot obtain it at your Chemist's, refuse Worthless Imitations, send 14 stamps, and it will be sent post free from

MACKENZIE'S CURE DEPOT READING.

own right, marketing an extensive range of pills, medicines and creams that they could supply from just one shop.

There were still some new patent medicinal products appearing and being promoted by chemists, doctors and others, such as Dr. Mackenzie's Catarrh-Cure Smelling Bottle, but drug manufacture and distribution was now becoming big business, with pharmaceutical companies widely using the Kent newspapers to promote their products, while a number of newspapers started printing their own medical, health or treatment advice columns.

It was in the second decade of the 20th century that a major step forward in medical treatment came into being with the passing of the NATIONAL HEALTH INSURANCE ACT, 1911. The Medical Benefits of this Act commenced on January 15th, 1913, whereby every insured person became entitled to Professional Advice, Medicine, and certain Surgical Appliances, without charge. The insured, having obtained a Prescription from his doctor, could take it to any Chemist they chose, provided that the Chemist was on the Dispensing Panel. But more about this in the following chapter.

Many of the advances in medicine and hospital treatment emanating from developments during the late 19th and early 20th century certainly lead to much better treatment of the wounded on the Western Front during World War I and again during World War II. These advances included aseptic surgery, the use of X-rays and being able to give blood transfusions.

The 20th century, as will be seen, was undoubtedly a quite remarkable period for medical advancements, with many discoveries and innovations changing the face of medicine and hospital operations, and improving the health and well-being of millions of people. Some of the most notable medical advancements of the 20th century included Alexander Fleming's discovery of penicillin in 1929 – the first antibiotic which could kill bacteria and treat infections – so revolutionising the treatment of diseases such as tuberculosis, pneumonia, syphilis, and meningitis.

Other key advances, which had their beginnings in the last decade of the 1800s (mentioned in earlier chapters and above) and into the early 1900s, included, as previously discussed, antiseptic and aseptic surgery, the discovery and development of X-rays and electrical therapy, the use of UV radiation, successful blood transfusions, the production of Adrenalin, and the first man-made antibiotics. Some of these discoveries and developments are briefly amplified further in the following pages and chapters.

ADVERTISING OF MEDICINES AND PILLS BECOMES MORE ELABORATE

By the middle of the first decade of the 1900s, the leading manufactures of medicines were stepping up their advertising in

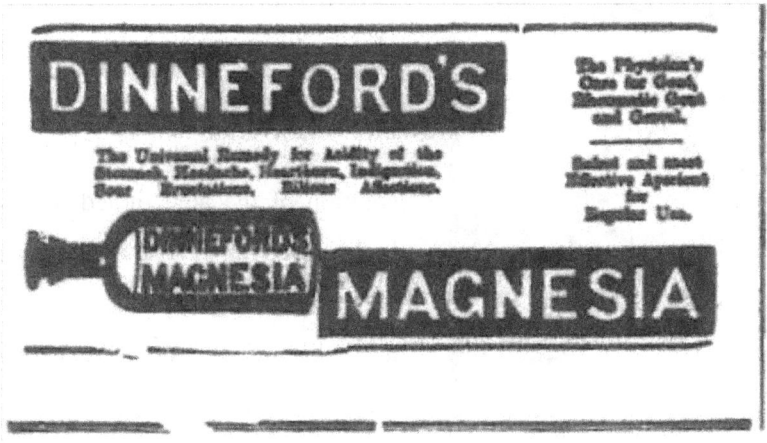

Kent newspapers, with more elaborate promotions by many of the leading players that had originally started their promotion in the 1800s, even as far back as the late 1700s. Drug manufacturers such as Beecham's Pills, Clarke's, Holloway's Pills and Ointment, Kaye's Wordsell's Pills, Vance's Balsam, Dinneford's Magnesia (as recommended and used by all good nurses), some of which have already featured in earlier pages, but now with logos or illustrations of their products.

Examples of some of these more detailed advertisements can be seen illustrated, on this and subsequent pages with two from just one page in the *Sheerness Guardian* and *East Kent Advertiser* in August 1903 and another from the *Kent Times* in October 1906.

A TURNING POINT IN THE HISTORY OF SURGERY

There can be little doubt that Joseph Lister's use of antiseptic surgery was a significant turning point in the history of surgery. This had come about in 1867 following his discovery that carbolic spray proved very effective in stopping wounds from getting gangrene. By spraying medical instruments, catgut and bandages with a 1-in-20 solution of the acid, it led to the better removal of bacteria around wounds and on surgical instruments and substantially reduced the death rate from infection.

Although some surgeons were critical of what Lister was doing, others were soon copying his methods and by the late 1800s and into the 1900s, successful appendectomies and other operations were being carried out, as well as the first cardiac surgery to repair a heart that had been damaged by a stab wound.

Lister's antiseptic surgery was to then lead the way for the introduction of aseptic surgery in the later years of the 19th century and early 20th century. Aseptic surgery ensured operating theatres were germ-free environments by ensuring that operating theatres and hospitals were continuously cleaned; that all surgical instruments were steam-sterilised to kill all bacteria; and surgeons wore rubber gloves, surgical gowns and masks that had been sterilised.

THE USE OF X-RAYS TO IDENTIFY BROKEN BONES

By the early 20th century, the discovery of X-rays by Wilhelm Röntgen, who had found that the rays could pass through paper, wood and human flesh, but not through metal or bone, was enabling surgeons to look inside their patients before an operation took place, with X-ray machines being used in hospitals to identify broken or splintered bones and locate dislocated joints.

Reports and advertisements regarding X-rays were already starting to appear in Kent newspapers by the end of the 1800s – such

The New Photography.

RONTGEN X RAYS.

YOUR SKELETON,

In Hands, Feet, & Arms, Revealed

Shadowgrams Taken by Appointment.

J. N. WILLIS,

OPERATOR.

3, MANOR ROAD, GRAVESEND

as the one shown here from the *Gravesend Reporter*, *North Kent and South Essex Advertiser* on 17th October 1896 – with photographers offering to take X-ray pictures of your skeleton in hands, feet and arms.

More X-ray stories appeared regularly in Kent newspapers right to the very end of the 1800s. Few were perhaps as extraordinary as the report that appeared in the *Westerham Herald* of 5th March 1898, which was headed THE X RAYS FOR A MURDERER. This went on to state that 'Before mounting the gallows, Charles Merry, a pedlar, under sentence of death at Chicago for wife murder, is to undergo an X-ray examination of his brain.' Apparently he had been struck on his head with a brick several years before, which had left a pronounced indentation.

His lawyers believed this to be partly responsible for the violent outbursts of temper which he showed. It was to learn the exact extent of the injury that the X-ray experiment was to be made, with a view to obtaining clemency from the Government. No mention can be found as to whether the X-ray appeal was successful or not.

In another report in the *Sheerness Guardian* and *East Kent Advertiser* in March 1897, it was noted that X-rays had been used to locate a halfpenny coin that had been swallowed five months ago by a little girl named Annie S. Parr. She had been taken to the infirmary

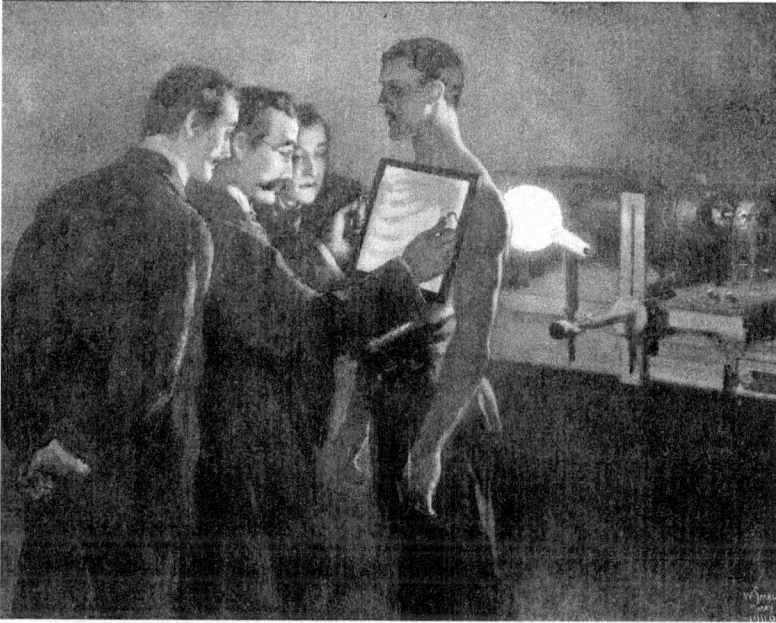

An early illustration of a Boer War soldier being examined in a London Hospital by means of X-ray. Illustration courtesy of Chronicle/Alamy Stock Photo

and photographed under X-ray, the location of the coin discovered, and an operation speedily and successfully performed. A few hours after, the little girl was said to be sitting up in bed playing with toys.

This ability to identify metal 'foreign objects' such as pieces of metal from shrapnel shells or bullets, and locate broken bones, was to become of huge benefit once the technology was trialled and successfully used on soldiers from the Boer War and then the Western Front during World War I.

However, not everything went well with X-rays. It was not long before Kent newspapers were writing about X-ray victims and even X-ray deaths, with scores of X-ray operators reportedly suffering from an incurable disease which was proving fatal as direct result of the manipulation of X-rays on the hands of the operators. This report from the *Westerham Herald* of 22nd October 1904, conveys the dangers admirably.

'A fortnight ago, a well-known doctor, who is in charge of the X-ray department at one of the largest of the London hospitals, had the first two joints of the forefinger of his right hand amputated, and last week it was found necessary to take the remainder of it away. "You can see from the fingers of the right hand how the trouble has developed," he remarked to an interviewer. The hand seemed as though it had been severely scalded. It was covered with an ulcerous eruption, and the nails looked as though they had been crushed and torn to pieces. "Have you suffered much pain during the progress of the malady." The doctor's face clouded over at the recollection of his sufferings. "My dear sir," he said. "I have suffered torments from last June onward, until I had my finger amputated. I scarcely knew what sleep was. Night after night I rolled about in agony. All the earlier workers," proceeded the doctor, "are suffering in greater or less degree; and this is due solely to the fact that we did not know what we were working with, and took no precautionary methods against possible danger." Mr. Harry Cox, of Rosebery-avenue, who supplies the Admiralty and the War Office with X-ray apparatus, was noted as another of the victims. He carries his left arm in a sling as the result of his injuries.

As a result of such problems with X-rays, regulations were drawn up by the British Protection Committee and engineers that provided for the enclosure of the apparatus in lead and the provision of all

110

necessary personal protective equipment to protect operators from scattered radiation, including the wearing of aprons, glasses, gloves and thyroid screens incorporating lead to reduce radiation exposure during X-ray examinations. Today, X-ray images of all areas of the human body are successfully taken every day, adding significantly to diagnosis and treatment.

ELECTRO MEDICAL APPARATUS AND ELECTROTHERAPEUTIC TREATMENTS

By the 1930s, hospitals are already incorporating not only X-ray equipment but rooms where other forms of electro-medical work is undertaken, including electrotherapeutic treatment and ultra-violet therapy. In a report in the *Sevenoaks Chronicle and Kentish Advertiser* in July 1934, it prints a considerable amount of detail about the newly-opened Kent and Sussex Hospital, some of which is summarized below.

This talks about a new department in which there is a 'large room where all electro-medical work is carried. The apparatus there converts the supply of current into a suitable form which passes through the body. There is also apparatus in which electric lamps or electric heating elements are mounted in such a way that the light and heat, produced by them can be applied to the body. Ultra violet radiation is produced by means of arc lamps in which electric current is converted into a radiation which one cannot perceive by the eyes, but which strongly affects the skin and so under proper control produces beneficial results.'

The report then continues with 'Also in this room there are machines which convert electrical current into a form which, although it can be passed in so large a quantity through the body without any electrical sensation whatever. The body is heated up Just like the filament of an electric lamp or the radiating element of an electric stove. These are known as diathermy machines. '

The report also mentions that the hospital has a number of rooms devoted to X-ray diagnosis and X-ray therapy. The first is the casualty room, where there is simple equipment intended to deal with the easiest and at the same time the most frequent cases calling for diagnosis — accidents and embedded foreign bodies like needles, etc. The unit delivers Just as much X-radiation as is necessary to see either the broken bones or the foreign bodies on a fluorescent screen, and make a record of them on a film. Two rooms are devoted to the therapeutic use of X-rays, while the main diagnostic room carries out examination of all patients who suffer from more serious complaints than a broken bone or embedded needle.

A few years later the *Sheerness Times Guardian* of the 4th January 1946, talks about the invention of the "Electric Knife" used in surgical operations which reduces the risk of infection, bleeding and shock.

In the same issue it writes about Diathermic Therapy, which produces heat inside the body for the relief of pain and the treatment of various diseases, explaining that a strong high frequency alternating electric current produces heat by the resistance it encounters; but passes through the human body without causing ill effects.

A still more recent method, it notes, is to make use of very short wireless waves of only a few metres instead of hundreds of metres long. Both the methods create, it writes, internal heat and a greater flow of blood without doing the patient any harm. They were said to be used for a variety of infections, arthritis, skin complaints, boils and carbuncles, chest troubles, inflammation of the eye, and so forth.

THE MATCHING OF BLOOD GROUPS AND SUCCESSFUL TRANSFUSIONS

One of the key problems with performing operations, amputations and being able to saves lives in previous centuries was due to blood loss, which could soon lead to a patient dying. This problem of blood loss was to be eventually overcome in the early 1900s when an Austrian, Karl Landsteiner, discovered that people could have different blood groups and that some blood groups were incompatible with another. Using his discovery he was able to show that blood transfusions would only work if the blood was compatible, explaining that each blood cell contained antibodies that reacted against the antibodies from a different blood group.

This discovery meant that if a patient and potential donor were a match and were in the same room, it was possible to undertake a successful blood transfusion. The patient needed to be in the same room because it was not possible to collect and store blood because it would clot. This had been the problem when blood transfusions had been previously tried, which had usually ended up killing the patient when different blood groups had been mixed, resulting in clotting. Matching blood groups stopped this happening.

Early stories of blood transfusion found in Kent newspapers of the early 1900s provide some quite extraordinary accounts, such as one that appeared in the *Sheerness Guardian and East Kent Advertiser* on August 16th 1902. This writes about a man named Simpson, who was nearly dead from consumption, when a Dr.

Hopkins, who was attending him, decided to try a transfusion of blood. As none of his friends or neighbours were willing to shed blood, the doctor had no alternative but to use a goat for the purpose, injecting about two quarts of the goat's blood into the patients arm, upon which he immediately began to revive – albeit with some disagreeable symptoms.

The report went on to say that no sooner had the patient's strength returned than he jumped out of bed, and twitching his head like a goat, butted the doctor three or four times in the stomach with the force of a battering ram, at which the doctor took refuge in an adjoining room. However, the patient then continued to butt the door with force. Unfortunately his mother-in-law entered the room and with one well-decided blow Simpson floored the old lady; as she lay screaming for help, he frolicked around her, making efforts to nibble green flower patterns in the carpet.

Distressed by the patients condition the doctor tried to undo the evil by bribing an Irishman, procuring blood, and injecting Simpson a second time. The report ended with saying that the man is now quite well, but speaks with an Irish brogue, and only butting once since the second transfusion. In this instance, it reported that Simpson was in church when one of the remaining corpuscles of the goat's blood got into his brain, whereupon he butted the Sexton half-way up the aisle. Fortunately he quickly recovered himself in time to apologise to the Sexton, but only just as the Sexton was about to floor him with a hymn book.

Like some of the other medical and medicinal developments from the late 1800s and early 1900s, World War I was to act as a key catalyst for the rapid development of blood banks and transfusion techniques, eventually leading to the National Blood Transfusion Service being set up in Britain in 1938. Again, more of this later.

HORMONES AND MAN-MADE ANTIBIOTICS

Prior to the 20th century the treatment of infections had been primarily-based on traditional and historical folklore, using mixtures with antimicrobial properties to treat infections. This was all about to change.

The early 1900s were to see the development by Japanese chemist, Jōkichi Takamine, of the first synthesized hormone, Adrenalin (also known as Epinephrine), a medicine used to treat several conditions, including allergic reaction anaphylaxis, cardiac arrest, and superficial bleeding.

One of the first reports on the discovery of Adrenalin can be found in the *Canterbury Journal, Kentish Times* and *Farmer's Gazette* of the 8th July 1905. The report notes that the discovery turned out to be one of the important discoveries in surgical chemistry, writing that 'adrenalin drives away the blood from any living tissue to which it is applied, so making it especially useful in delicate surgery, especially of the nose and throat.'

The report went on to state that 'formerly, an operation in the nasal passages was followed by a rush of blood. Now the surface can be treated with adrenalin and it can be cut like fresh meat.' It also noted that 'it is the most powerful heart stimulant known. Surgeons inject it into patients dying from the shock of operations, where it then drives the blood ahead of it, giving the heart a quick squeeze, which will sometimes start it going, even after it has practically stopped.' It concluded with saying that adrenalin is rather a costly drug, however, since the process of manufacture from the glands of sheep is long and delicate.

The discovery of adrenalin was followed in 1907 with the synthesizing by Alfred Bertheim of Arsphenamine, one of the early man-made antibiotics, and with the first modern antibiotic that could kill bacteria and treat infections being discovered by Paul Ehrlich two years later in 1909.

The best known – and first commercialised – antibiotic, penicillin, was discovered by Alexander Fleming in 1928. Since then, there have been many new antibiotics discovered, but also sadly many new types of bacteria have also appeared that are resistant to them. Nevertheless, antibiotics have been able to drastically change modern medicine and extended average life expectancy by more than 20 years over the past 100 years.

EVER MORE PROMOTIONS FOR ARTIFICIAL TEETH AND DENTISTRY

Mentioned was made in a previous chapter that advertising had started to be placed in Kent newspapers by dentists for the making and fitting of false teeth. The early years of the 1900s sees even more of such advertising, with adverts being placed for artificial teeth, teeth remodelling, lifelike teeth with suction plates from 20 shillings, stoppings, and extractions. This can be seen in these advertisements placed in the *Sheerness Times and General Advertiser* in December 1905 by Macdonald's Teeth and by W. L. Barrett, both in Sheerness, together with an advertisement by G. Arrowsmith, Surgeon Dentist, in the *Herne Bay Press* in September 1900.

Interestingly, the Arrowsmith advertisement promotes their Enamelled Artificial Teeth, which are noted as being specially renowned for use, comfort, durability and their life-like natural appearance, and also noting that tooth extractions were one shilling per tooth, while consultations were free.

NEWSPAPERS NOW CARRY HEALTH OR MEDICAL ADVICE COLUMNS

Kent newspapers now not only carried advertisements by drug companies, chemists, doctors and dentists, by many also started to have regular weekly advice column to explain the benefits of healthy eating, good digestion – even on how to choose artificial limbs – as can be seen from the following article in the *Westerham Herald* in December 1900, headed THE DIGESTION.

This column went on to say 'Much can be done towards inducing firm, healthy flesh by attention to diet; and those who are too thin can, with little expense and effort, overcome this trouble.' then continuing with 'Olive oil is one of the most nutritious of food products, and a persistent and liberal use of salads aids materially in the acquisition of flesh. A salad of orange and bananas, cut in small pieces, and liberally supplied with French salad dressing, will never harm the digestive organs.'

The article also noted that 'Vegetable salads should be freely indulged in at luncheon and dinner, with plenty of good salad oil. Fish salads are excellent and sardines form a valuable addition to the "beauty" bill of fare. Milk is flesh-forming, so are grapes and raisins. Exercise the chest as much as possible, and friction well, also, the arms with a soft towel. Honey is flesh-forming, and a very wholesome article it is; indeed, for human consumption no article can be found more delicious than honey, and none more beneficial to health. Take it on toast or bread and butter, while it is delicious with suet puddings and dumplings. Sleep and rest all possible, avoid undue excitement, simply take things calmly, and be happy.'

Another article in the same newspaper was headed ARTIFICIAL LIMBS. This went on to say that 'People who buy artificial limbs from good makers must be prepared to expend a lot of money. The best legs sold generally cost as much as £16. It is not, however, necessary to pay such a high price as this. A very efficient, serviceable limb can be obtained for two-thirds of the money. A leg for use when amputation has taken place below the knee is naturally costly. A complete arm, with which goes a set of instruments to screw into the palm of the hand, costs £12. A less highly finished one may be bought for £8, and for cases of amputation below the elbow, in the two qualities, £4 less in the case of either will purchase the required substitute.'

An interesting editorial in the *Sheerness Times Guardian* in December 1908 was headed NO NEED FOR MEDICINE. This stated that Medicines may be left out of account in treating dyspepsia on rational lines. In some cases, to be determined only by a qualified medical man, they may prove of some temporary use as palliatives, but the cure will have to go much deeper. There are thousands of persons who have ruined their digestive organs for life by the drugs they have taken for other maladies; but it would probably be hard to find a dozen persons who were cured of their dyspepsia by the use of drug remedies. Statements may not harmonise with the cunningly-worded patent medicine advertisements and the faked-up testimonials that occupy so much space in the Press; nevertheless, it is true. The report was signed 'Ellsworth.'

Many other example of health or medical advice columns can be found in early 1900s Kent newspapers, some of course even extending such columns into the 20th and 21st centuries.

KENT HOSPITALS AND THE IMPACT OF WORLD WAR I

As can be seen from these pages, medicines, medical treatments, X-rays, blood transfusions, antibiotics and adrenalin had transformed life expectancy, operation outlooks and health quite dramatically during the late 1800s and the early years of the 1900s. But it was not just these developments that were having an impact. Hospitals had been, and were being, built in Kent towns, with large General Hospitals in the major towns and smaller Cottage Hospitals in many of the smaller towns, as well as Isolation Hospitals, Small Pox Hospitals and Nursing Homes. In addition, there were a number of Military Hospitals for British and Canadian forces in Kent, all of which were extremely busy during World War I.

Just perusing the early 1900 Kent newspapers finds information about the following:

Kent and Canterbury Hospital

Ramsgate General Hospital

Maidstone Hospital

Tunbridge Wells General Hospital (50 in patients and some 500 out-patients during 1913)

Tonbridge Hospital

Ashford Cottage Hospital

Victoria Cottage Hospital, Deal

Shorncliffe Military Hospital

Bevan Military Hospital, Sandgate

Faversham Hospital

Eastbridge Hospital, Canterbury

St. Bartholomew's Hospital, Rochester

Royal Victoria Hospital, Folkestone

Fernleigh Hospital, Larkfield

Herne Bay Cottage Hospital

Hawkhurt Cottage Hospital

Dunsdale Hospital, Westerham

Otford Isolation Hospital

Sittingbourne Hospital

Faversham and Whitstable Nursing Homes

Canterbury Small Pox Hospital, Trenley Park Green

Gravesend Hospital

A report in the *Faversham News* in March 1911, headed THE HOSPITALS provided the following information: 'The Executive and Appeals Sub-Committees, reporting for the period 1st September to 30th November, 1910, stated that arrangements had been made for the treatment of discharged disabled men at the Cottage Hospital, Margate, and the Holmesdale Cottage Hospital, Sevenoaks, while Rosemary Convalescent Home, Herne Bay, was opened on the 8th October, and several cases had been accommodated there. At the suggestion of the Ministry of Pensions, in response to a request from the owner, it had been decided not to proceed with the establishment of the proposed new hospital at The Hawthorns, Chislehurst. As regards Swanton House, Ashford, it was understood that H.M. Office of Works was proceeding with the equipment of' these premises as a hospital. Dr. Grogono, Herne Bay, and Dr. Watson, Sheerness, had been appointed Medical Referees.'

KENT HOSPITALS DURING THE 1914-1918 WAR

There are many reports in Kent newspapers in the period from 1900 to the 1920s and 1930s which provide some interesting snapshots of hospital life during this period, particularly during the War years. The Gravesend Yacht Club, for example, was lent as a hospital during World War I, with no fewer than 1,350 wounded soldiers being helped through the hospital to convalesce.

The Elham Union Workhouse at Eachend Hill, Lyminge, was taken over as a whole by the Canadian military authorities who required the building for the treatment of patients suffering venereal disease. The existing patients were transferred to other Workhouses in Kent, including Tenterden, Hollingbourne and Eastry.

Another report noted that 'Everything was done to make the wounded soldiers at the Mount Hospital, Faversham (used at one time as the Office of the Ministry of National Insurance and now a Grade II Listed Building), have a happy time. The lounge and hail were decorated, and turkey and plum pudding provided for dinner. A large number of friends sent gifts. On Christmas evening there was a concert, on Boxing Day a dance, and on Sunday night another concert.

The Mount Hospital had appeared in other Kent newspaper reports during the War, noting that it was generously placed at the disposal of the military for one year, rent free, by the Executors of the late Mr. P. B. Neame, and has been fitted up as a hospital by the members of the Faversham Nursing Division and St. John Ambulance Brigade, zealously assisted by other willing workers. 'We are now in a position to take in 40 patients (wounded officers and men). All this done by loans and gifts.' The Mount, owing to its commodious and pleasant situation, was said to make an ideal hospital.

CHRISTMAS CELEBRATIONS

There are also frequent reports about hospital Christmas celebrations taking place in Kent Hospitals, some of which – from the *Faversham Times and Mercury* in January 1915 – are documented below:

'There were five patients at the Faversham Cottage Hospital and on Christmas Day they were allowed to have their friends to tea. The dinner was generously provided by Mr and Mrs Rigden and Miss Rigden sent a gift of sweets.

At Kennaway's Hospital there were also five patients, three adults and two children, all of whom were sufficiently well enough to partake of the Christmas fare provided. Gifts were sent by the Mayor and Mayoress and Mrs. Anderson.

At Beacon Hill there were no less than 54 patients, all children, but they were nearly all convalescent, and able to spend a very happy time. A Christmas tree and a gramophone were the chief items of the Programme. Gift's were sent by Dr. and Mrs. Alexander, Dr. Selby, the Vicar of Teynham and Mrs. Parton, and the members of the Rural District Council.

Although not at actually at Christmas, an interesting report in the *Tonbridge Free Press* of 6th November, 1931, provided information on the provision of hospital food at The Tonbridge Hospital, with the Hospital Sub-Committee reporting that the cost of food for the patients and staff for the month of September had worked out at 1s. 6¼d. per head per day, compared with 1s. 3¼. for the previous month.

SOME INTERESTING KENT HOSPITAL INSIGHTS

An interesting item in the *Folkestone, Hythe, Sandgate & Cheriton*

Herald in October 1910, noted that there was a great deal of misunderstanding regarding Folkestone Hospital, in which it appeared that if a Cheriton school child suffering from adenoids and tonsils went to Folkestone Hospital, even if they had a letter for admission, that child could not be treated because the honorary physicians and surgeons refused to see the child.

It turned out that the reason for this difficulty was that a clinic had been established in Folkestone for school children to go to for attention from a doctor for adenoids and tonsils, Folkestone children were therefore not treated at the Hospital but received their treatment at the Clinic, which was run by the Folkestone Education Committee, whereas Cheriton came within the Elham Rural District of the Kent Education Committee and they had no provision for treatment to be made. It was decided that the County Medical Officer should be asked to resolve this matter.

In March 1911, the *Faversham News* in March 1911 reported that the Faversham Hospital report book had noted that there were six patients at the present time. During the month four had been admitted and three discharged. The Matron wrote asking that a bath might be provided for the nurses. At present they had to use one that was used by the patients. It appeared that the provision of a bath meant also the provision of a bathroom, or the addition of another bedroom if one that is at present reserved for an extra nurse was converted into a bathroom. It was resolved that the Hospital Committee should visit and report.

A report in the *South Eastern Gazette* on the 28th December, 1915, reported that 'A reply was read from the Hollingbourne Rural

District Council agreeing with the Maidstone Hospital Committee Clerk's suggestions as to the impropriety of persons, after accompanying patients to the Hospital, travelling back in a public conveyance.' The letter added that those persons should be asked to submit themselves to disinfection, and asked the Council's opinion as to the desirability of providing a motor ambulance, in which the Hollingbourne Council were ready to co-operate. The suggestion of the Hollingbourne Authority was referred to the Hospital Committee.

20TH CENTURY LEGISLATION BRINGS CONTROLS AND BENEFITS FOR ALL

Up until the early 1900s there was not any kind of health service to help people who became ill or who had developed a long-term disabling sickness, were injured at work or in an accident, who found themselves unemployed or through being unable to work in old age. Most of the poor in society could not afford to pay a doctor or pay for any kind of medical treatment.

Poverty was undoubtedly a major concern in Britain at this time and many working class and poor in society would even struggle to pay for over-the-counter medications costing a shilling or less. Overall, the working class were deemed as having a rather poor physical condition, lived in overcrowded conditions, and generally had a poor or inadequate diet.

Those in the population that did manage to pay for over-the-counter medicines, pills or potions at the local chemist shop or grocery store had no guarantee that the medications – still uncontrolled in the early 1900s – would be effective, did not contain any kind of poison, or could contain strong opioids that might lead them into drug addiction.

Indeed, there were still many pharmacies and other outlets selling or dispensing patent or own product medications, with no regulations or any kind of control over their manufacture, testing (if any), marketing messages, claimed effectiveness or use. Indeed, drugs incorporating opium, morphine, heroin and coca were relatively commonplace and widely used in almost all levels of society. It was not until the 1920s that Regulations were introduced to regulate the claims made on drug labels,

127

with pharmaceutical companies finally being required to prove the safety of their drugs – although not yet their efficacy.

Then, in the 1930s, further regulations were introduced covering the manufacture, sale, possession and use of medicines and poisons.

The most significant advances in healthcare were to come in 1911 and 1948, with, first, the introduction of the National Health Insurance Act, 1911, and then The National Health Service Act introduced on the 5th of July 1948, by the Minister of Health, Aneurin Bevan. This later Act was to provide healthcare that was free for all at the point of delivery. More about this later.

Kent newspapers of course followed all these developments and Acts of Parliament in their pages right through the years of 1911 to 1948, bringing healthcare into a modern world after several hundred years of virtually uncontrolled medicines, unregulated use of poisons and opiates, and with few limits on the reporting of widely exaggerated healthcare successes.

The following pages look at some of these development in rather more detail, with input from Kent newspapers from the early 1900s reporting on how they were implemented.

COMPULSORY HEALTH INSURANCE INTRODUCED

It was not until the second decade of the 20th century that the first major step forward in medical treatment in England came into being. The NATIONAL HEALTH INSURANCE ACT, 1911, introduced an important piece of social legislation that was passed by the Liberal Government to protect working people against loss of income if they were sick or unemployed.

The Act created a national system of health insurance and unemployment insurance, with compulsory health insurance contributions coming from employers (who paid 4d,), the government (who paid 2d.), and workers earning under £160 per year (who paid 3d.) If the employee became ill, they would be paid 9 shillings (for up to 13 weeks) and then 5 shillings (for an additional; 13 weeks). The employee was also offered free medical treatment. However, the benefit was lost after 26 weeks absence from work, with the Poor Law being left to provide for the worker.

THE NATIONAL INSURANCE ACT 1911

BEING A TREATISE ON THE SCHEME OF NATIONAL HEALTH INSURANCE AND INSURANCE AGAINST UNEMPLOYMENT CREATED BY THAT ACT, WITH THE INCORPORATED ENACTMENTS, FULL EXPLANATORY NOTES TABLES AND EXAMPLES

BY

ORME CLARKE
OF THE INNER TEMPLE AND WESTERN CIRCUIT, BARRISTER-AT-LAW

WITH AN INTRODUCTION
BY

SIR JOHN SIMON, K.C.V.O., M.P.
SOLICITOR-GENERAL

" The beauty of laws for human creatures is their adaptability to new stitchings." THE LANCET, chap. xviii.

LONDON:
BUTTERWORTH & CO., 11 & 12, BELL YARD, TEMPLE BAR.
Law Publishers.
GLASGOW AND EDINBURGH:
WILLIAM HODGE & COMPANY.

1912

Aimed at removing the stigma of the Poor Law and designed to help workers, it was to become one of the key foundations of the modern welfare state.

The Medical Benefits of this Act commenced on January 15th, 1913, whereby every insured person became entitled to 'Professional Advice, Medicine, and certain Surgical Appliances, without charge.' The insured, having obtained a Prescription from his doctor, could take it to any Chemist they chose, provided that the Chemist was on the Dispensing Panel.

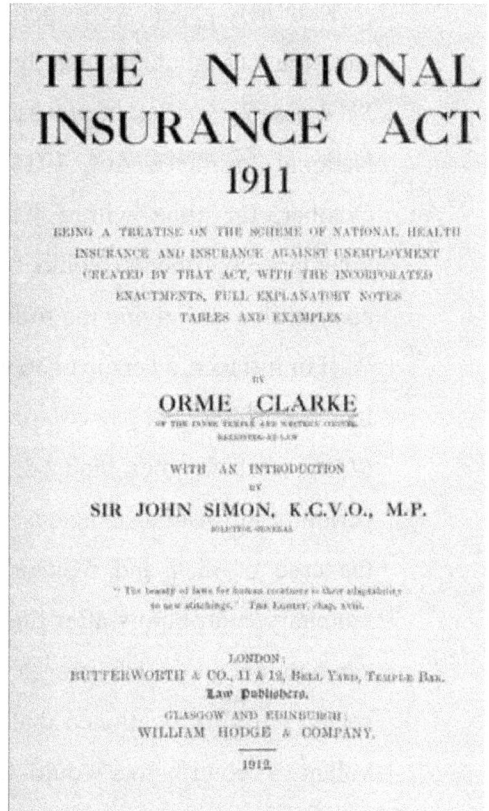

Kent newspapers were soon active in advising readers about the Act, the contributions and benefits. On 4th October 1913, the *Sheerness Times Guardian* was drawing attention to the fact that the National Insurance Act, 1913, had been extended to the 12th October, the time within which persons qualified to become voluntary contributors could become insured at reduced rates of contribution and giving the following example:

'For instance, a person of 36 who becomes a voluntary contributor before that date will pay contributions at the ordinary employed rate (7d. a week for men, and 6d. a week for women) for the whole period of his insurance, against 9d. and 8d. payable, respectively, in the case of men and women of that age becoming insured as voluntary contributors after the date mentioned. An insured person can only obtain the advantages of insurance by joining an approved society.' It also mentioned that a leaflet explaining the position of voluntary contributors could be obtained on application to the Secretary, National Health Insurance Commission (England), Buckingham Gate, London.

Chemists and pharmacies also started to advertise their services in the dispensing of National Health Insurance prescriptions, such as one placed in the *Whitstable Times and Herne Bay Herald* in January 1914 by Walker and Harris Ltd, Cash Chemists, in Harbour Street, Whitstable. This advised that insured persons bringing their prescription to them would have a prompt and active service, with courtesy. All prescriptions will be dispensed, checked and finished in the best style and under the personal supervision of a fully qualified Dispensing Chemist. It also noted that 'If desired, medicines will be sent to any address by Special Messenger, free of charge, thus ensuring a considerable saving of time to the person bringing the prescription.'

In another example, the *Deal, Walmer & Sandwich Mercury* in April 1914, ran an advertisement by Stewart Dunn, M.P.S. Pharmacist, 96 and 100 High Street, Deal, stating that prescriptions would be dispensed with accuracy and promptness, free of charge. Many other examples can be found in newspapers throughout Kent.

CONTROL AND REGULATION OF MEDICINES, OPIOIDS AND POISONS.

While major advances were taking place in all kinds of medical treatments and dentistry in the early 1900s, medicines, pills, creams, elixirs and other healthy living products were still being widely advertised and promoted, including all the usual extravagant claims and testimonials found in the Kentish newspapers right up until 1912. Drug use in England at this time was still largely uncontrolled and drugs incorporating opium, morphine, heroin and coca were relatively commonplace and widely used.

Then, prior to the First World War, Britain signed the International Opium Convention at The Hague in 1912. This imposed stricter controls on doctors and pharmacists in relation to dangerous drugs and committed countries to preventing trade in morphine, opium and cocaine. A few years later, in 1916, the army council enacted the Defence of the Realm Act regulation (an emergency legislation-making powers during wartime), to prohibit the sale of cocaine and opium to troops. This legislation was subsequently widened to criminalise civilian possession of those drugs without a medical need.

131

It was not until the provisions of the Dangerous Drugs Acts of 1920 (again incorporated under the Defence of the Realm Act regulations). and again in 1923 were introduced that the regulation and distribution of opioid and illicit supplies were fully controlled; a policy maintained in Britain right up until the 1960s. The Act established that medical practitioners were allowed to prescribe morphine, cocaine and heroin. Subsequent legislation has been introduced over the years.

Reaction to the passing of the Act included the following report found in the *Westerham Herald* in September 1920, headed DANGEROUS DRUGS. ENDEAVOUR TO PUT A STOP TO THE HABIT. The report explained that The Dangerous Drugs Act, which was now in force, had been designed to put a stop to the drug habit, which had grown rapidly in the last few years. The report noted that, in future, licences will be required for the import and export of opium, medicinal opium, morphia, cocaine, diamorphine (heroin), and ecgonine, and stating that the prohibition also extended to salts of morphine, diamorphine, cocaine, ecgonine, and preparations, dilutions or extracts in which these drugs were used.

It went on to say that Import licences would be issued by the Home Office and Export licences by the Board of Trade, and that holders of import licences under the cocaine and opium proclamation would be required to apply for new licences. London and Liverpool were to be the only ports through which raw opium could be imported and exported, while the manufacture, sale, or possession of opium prepared for smoking was prohibited.

There are numerous reports in Kent newspapers in the 1920s and

1930s, after the Act had been passed, of prosecutions for drug possession under the Dangerous Drugs Act, of drug smuggling, of refusing to supply the name of a person to whom drugs were supplied, or for being a supplier.

In one report in the *Kent and Sussex Courier* in September 1927, an Annie Maud Anderson was charged with attempting to obtain possession of a dangerous drug, namely a tube of morphine tablets, contrary to the Dangerous Drugs Act, at Tunbridge Wells by claiming to be a doctor. The accused elected to be dealt with summarily and pleaded guilty. In defence, she said that she had suffered from severe attacks of pain, which became so bad that she was unable to bear them. She admitted that she was not a doctor but had been a nurse some years ago. After some deliberation she was pronounced guilty and sentenced to three months imprisonment.

Regulations were also later introduced to regulate the claims made on drug labels, with pharmaceutical companies finally required to prove the safety of their drugs – although not yet the efficacy. Then in 1933, The Pharmacy and Poisons Act was passed in the United Kingdom; this regulated the manufacture, sale, possession and use of medicines and poisons. The main purpose of the Act was to protect the public from the dangers of unqualified and unregulated dispensing of drugs and chemicals.

The Act established a central authorit the Privy Council – to oversee the pharmacy profession and the Poisons List, which classified substances into two parts according to their toxicity and potential for misuse. The act also required that the sale of poisons be affected by or under the supervision of a registered or recognised pharmacist, and that the purchaser provide their name and address. The act also made membership of the Pharmaceutical Society of Great Britain compulsory for all registered pharmaceutical chemists and chemists and druggists.

BLOOD BANKS, TRANSFUSIONS AND TRANSPLANTS

The previous chapter talked about the discovery of distinct blood types and some of the early blood transfusions. To begin with, transfusions used whole blood that was injected intravenously. More common today is to use only components of the blood, such a red blood cells, white blood cells, plasma, platelets and other clotting platelets.

The National Blood Transfusion Service, initially introduced in 1938 and taken under the control of the Ministry of Health in 1946, has undoubtedly been a key element in saving the lives of thousands of people over the years that have followed. Blood banks, with blood

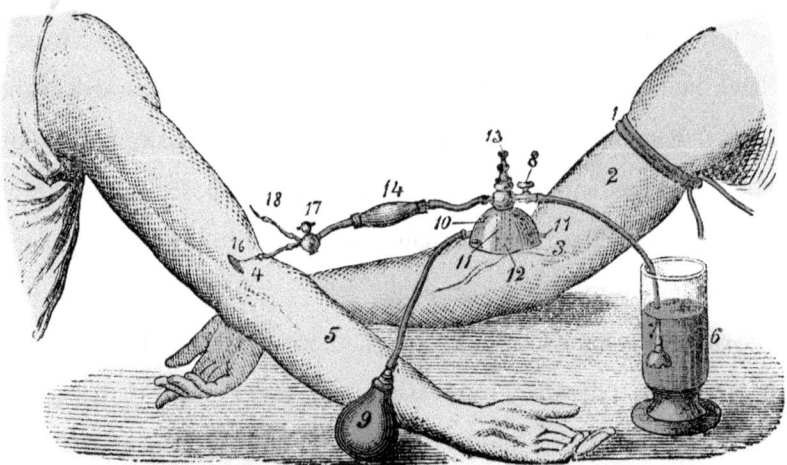

Early experimentation in blood transfusion between two people.
Illustration courtesy Science History Images/Alamy Stock Photo

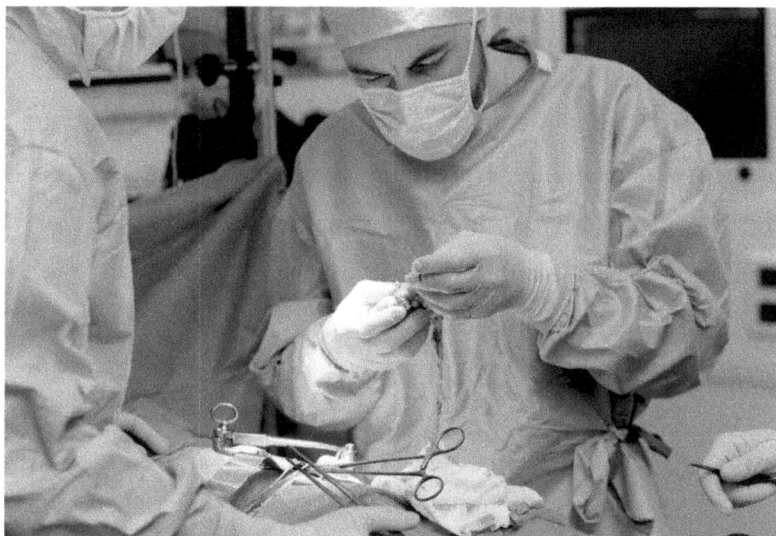

A more modern illustration of a kidney transplant taking place.
Illustration courtesy of BSIP/Alamy Stock Photo

provided on a large scale by volunteer donors, were created to meet the needs of injured Service personnel and civilians casualties during the Second World War.

Following on from the developments taking place in blood transfusions, came the initial successes in organ transplants. The first human organ to be transplanted (in 1954) was the kidney. By the late 1960s, liver, heart and pancreas transplants were all being successfully performed, followed in the 1980s with the beginnings of lung and intestinal organ transplants.

THE CHALLENGES OF PHARMACEUTICAL LABELLING IN THE MODERN AGE

Since the initial legislation in the first decades of the 1900s, further legislation and updates have been regularly introduced to cover the labelling of pharmaceutical/drug products. Today, legislation

135

provides more challenges to the drug manufacturers and the label/ packaging industry than almost any other market, both in terms of legislative requirements and in terms of the wide range of applications and solutions required. Overall, the pharmaceutical/drugs market is today made up of five main areas of application:

Primary labels for ethical drugs

Over-the-counter products

Prescription labels

Veterinary products

Sundry healthcare products.

Regulations on pharmaceutical/drug labelling now require labels to carry the name of the product, name and quantity of each active ingredient, strength and route of administration, name and address of the manufacturer, a registration or licence number, batch number, expiry date and any specific storage conditions. The regulations provide for the correct particulars to be included on each label at each stage in the distribution process; that the label is consistent with the provisions of the Product Licence; that all labelling is carried out in a way that is indelible, clear, legible and can be easily read by the purchaser.

Regulations may also require the inclusion in the packaging of all medicinal products of a package leaflet that contains information for users. This leaflet needs to include: the identification of the product, name of the product, a statement of active ingredients, the pharmaceutical form, the name and address of the holder, therapeutic indications, a list of information which is necessary before taking the product, necessary and usual instructions for use, a description of undesirable effects, a reference to the expiry date, the date the leaflet was last revised, any symbols or pictograms designed to clarify certain information

FREE HEALTHCARE FOR ALL

Probably the most significant of all the pieces of medical health, pharmacy, drugs and poisons legislation introduced in the first half of the 1900s, and mentioned earlier, was the National Health Services Act, passed by the new Labour Government in 1946 and which came into effect in July 1948.

The idea of national co-ordination of the health services and the supply of free medical care to all had been steadily gaining both popular and political support throughout much of the 1930s and early 1940s. Then, in 1944, a Ministry of Health (under a war-time coalition government) published a White Paper on a National Health Service, putting forward proposals for a system of free universal healthcare funded by taxation.

Following a landslide general election by the Labour Party in 1945, the National Health Service Act was passed in 1946 and, despite strong disagreement over the proposed service (between the government and the British Medical Association representing doctors) a workable system put together by the new Minister of Health, Aneurin Bevan, came into being on 5th July 1948, so providing healthcare that was free at the point of delivery.

With the passing of the Act and its implementation in 1948 it is perhaps not surprising that Kent Newspapers started to carry numerous reports relating to how the service would be implemented and administered in the County. Typical of the kinds of Kent newspaper reporting of the Act can be seen in the following extract that appeared in the *Thanet Advertiser* in January 1948.

Headed 'Health Proposals', the report went on to state that The Health Committee had been giving further consideration to the Kent County Council's proposals for the administration of health services under the National Health Services Act, 1946. The proposals provide for the setting up of area sub-committees on which district council's would be represented—Broadstairs representation being one member. The County Council proposed to delegate the administration of the health services to the area sub-committees and having considered the position in the light of the negotiations between the County Council and the Kent Borough and Urban District Councils' Association, the committee were raising no objections.

Not everything in relation to implementing the new Act seems to have gone well in the early months, with the *Kent & Sussex Courier* just one month later, in February 1948, running a heading stating The DOCTORS SAID 'NO', followed by a sub-heading that ran 'State Health Act Rejected Locally and Nationally.' The report went on to say that the BMA had published the figures of their recent plebiscite held among doctors in the country, which revealed the doctors' determination not to take service under the National Health Services Act as it stood, adding that eighty-two per cent of doctors voted, with the majority against accepting service.

Later in this report it presented the Doctors' case, put forward by Dr. A. M. Pollock, chairman of the Tunbridge Wells Division of the BMA, in which he stressed that members were convinced that the

Act would regiment them into Government services and that their capacity and desire for personal service would be endangered, adding that the declared policy of the Government was to introduce a full-time State salaried medical service.

It seems it was not just doctors that were against the Act; it was also dentists. A separate report in the same newspaper, stated that at a meeting of dental practitioners in Tunbridge Wells, Tonbridge and district, a unanimous vote was made against service under the Act in its present form, and claiming that the Act perpetuated the worst features of NHI dentistry, leading to the lowest possible standard of dentistry by removing incentives to dentists to reach high standards and acquire additional qualifications.

In another report in the *East Kent Times and Mail* of 13th March 1948, a special meeting of the honorary staff committee of the Ramsgate General Hospital had met and passed a unanimous resolution that members of the medical staff at the Hospital should not take service under the Act until agreement had been reached between the profession as a whole and the Government.

Similar reports of objections or concerns emanating from doctors, dentists, nurses, pharmacies, councils, health committees and others, can be found right through 1948 and onwards. A number of Councils in particular submitted concerns about the way the Kent County Council had submitted proposals regarding the carrying out of duties under the Act, with Margate Council placing on record its profound regret that sufficient opportunity was not given for it to discuss measures as provided under the Act.

Notwithstanding so many objections and concerns about the

workings and administration of the National Health Act, it was subsequently reported in the *Dover Express* in June 1948 that out of just over 600 doctors in Kent, 389 had so far Joined the National Health Service. In addition, 69 other doctors whose practices extend over the borders into Kent, had also joined.

By May 1949, the *Sheerness Times Guardian* was able to report that as a result of the National Health Services Act the Kent County Council now operated all the County's Ambulance, Home Help, Maternity and Childcare and Hospital Services.

A SAFER AND HEALTHIER COUNTY

After several hundred years of dubious medicines, quack doctors and unsafe hospital treatments and procedures, the later years of the 1800s and the first half of the 1900s had brought a revolution to the medical world in Kent. New Acts of Parliament covering poisons, drugs and the labelling of medicines, together with the introduction of antiseptic procedures, antibiotics and anaesthetics, X-rays and electrical therapies, blood transfusions, safer infection-free surgery, and then the commencement of a free for all National Health Services, had changed life expectancy and health in the County for the better.

At this point, it is probably a good time to bring this 300-year historical look at the medical and health history of Kent to a conclusion. A lot has changed for good in the health care of Kent's population since the later years of the 1600s. For this we should all be thankful.

Index of medications, treatments and suppliers

ACKNOWLEDGEMENTS

Researching and writing a book that looks at the history and evolution of medicines, pills, potions and the many advances in antiseptic and aseptic procedures, blood transfusions, X-rays, etc., and then the introduction of National Insurance and the National Health Service, particularly as they relate to Kent from the end of the 17th century right through to the mid 19th century has taken many hours, days and weeks of studying on-line page and advertisement archives found in both national and Kent newspapers, some of which first appear from as far back as 1726, most notably the *Kentish Weekly Post* or *Canterbury Journal*, and then the *Kentish Gazette*.

Later came a number of other local Kent newspapers that helped bring the county's medical and healthcare story up to the mid 1900s. These papers included the *East Kent Times and Mail*, the *Whitstable Times* and *Herne Bay Herald*, the *Tunbridge Wells Journal*, the *Kentish Express*, the *East Kent Gazette*, the *Tonbridge Free Press*, the *Gravesend Reporter, North Kent and South Essex Advertiser*, the *Sheerness Times Guardian, South Eastern Gazette, Faversham Times and Mercury, Gravesend and Northfleet Standard, Maidstone Journal and Kentish Advertiser*, The *Canterbury Journal, Dover Telegraph and Cinque Ports Advertiser, Folkestone Express, Gravesend Reporter, Westerham Herald, Sevenoaks Chronicle, Herne Bay Press, Faversham News*, and the *Thanet Advertiser*.

All these newspapers, as well as hundreds of others, are all now available for researchers and writers to subscribe to and study thanks to the work of The British Newspaper Archive. Acknowledgement and thanks are due to this invaluable resource – including all the newspapers mentioned – for permission to reproduce images of certain advertisements and text content in this book.

Finding suitable historical images and illustrations relating to the book content also proved to be possible through Alamy (registered as Alamy Limited) a British privately owned stock photography agency. Thanks are due to them for permission to use specific illustrations included in the book.

Others that need to be acknowledged are Bryan Trill, a long-time family friend, who read and commented on the original manuscript, made helpful suggestions and corrected spelling and grammar where required, together with Greg Smye-Rumsby of Concept Design who has once again worked on cover design and page format for one of the books in the Kent's Untold History Project series, as well as for other historical and biographical titles written by the same author.

ABOUT THE AUTHOR

Michael Fairley has written or contributed to more than 30 books in his forty-five year career as a lecturer, writer, author and publisher, including eleven historical or biographical titles, five international encyclopedias, and some 15 text or technical books.

Born in Kent, he has lived and worked or studied in Sittingbourne, Canterbury, Margate, Minster, Deal, Sandgate, and Hawkinge - where he now resides – and has travelled extensively throughout Europe, the Americas and Australia.

He has contributed to business-to-business magazines and journals worldwide, both as a contributor and editor, as well as being a well-established international keynote conference, seminar and workshops speaker.

Titles in the Kent's Untold History Project series of books by Michael Fairley that are now available are:

The Glorious days of Music Hall and Variety Theatre in Kent seaside resorts.
Available through Amazon Books

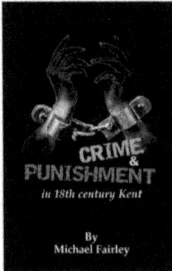

Crime & Punishment in 18th century Kent
Available through Amazon Books

Stagecoaches, Waggons, Roadside Inns and Highwaymen
Available through Amazon Books

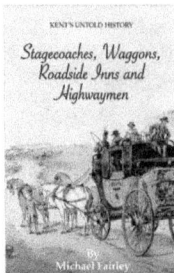

Sports and recreations of Kentish Gentlemen 1700-1900
Available through Amazon Books

Other historical or biographical titles by Michael Fairley include:

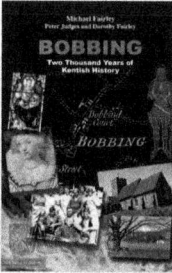

Bobbing – Two Thousand Years of Kentish History
Available from Sittingbourne Heritage Museum

One of life's great charmers. A biography of Charles Kay. Sporting legend, songwriter and well-love comedian.
Available through Amazon Books

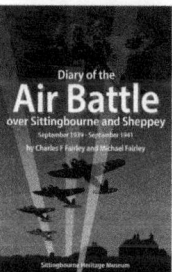

William Kay - Cotton manufacturer and liberal benefactor 1775 - 1846
Available through Amazon Books

Diary of the Air Battle over Sittingbourne and Sheppey. September 1939 - September 1941
Available from Sittingbourne Heritage Museum

Other historical or biographical titles by Michael Fairley include:

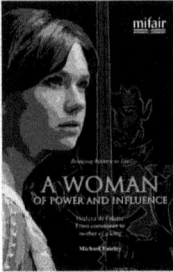

A woman of Power and Influence. Herleva de Falaise. From commoner to mother of a king

Available through Amazon Books

www.ingramcontent.com/pod-product-compliance
Lightning Source LLC
Chambersburg PA
CBHW071345090426
42738CB00012B/3013